Recuerdos

MEMORIES OF CHILDHOOD IN TUCSON

Nori—
Thanks for your friendship
+ helpful horse tips!
Beth

Recuerdos

MEMORIES OF CHILDHOOD IN TUCSON

Elizabeth McCauslin

SYREN BOOK COMPANY
Minneapolis

Most Syren Books are available at special quantity discounts for bulk purchases for sales promotions, premiums, fund-raising, and educational needs. For details, write

Syren Book Company
Special Sales Department
5120 Cedar Lake Road
Minneapolis, Minnesota 55416

Published by
Syren Book Company LLC
5120 Cedar Lake Road
Minneapolis, Minnesota 55416

Printed in the United States of America on acid-free paper

ISBN 0-929636-41-4

LCCN 2005920306

Book design and production by MIGHTY MEDIA.

Cover art: Juan L. Cota, 1972, Painting of Terrazas home, 591 S. Stone Ave.

This book was typeset using *Hoefler Text* and *Knockout* typefaces from HOEFLER TYPE FOUNDRY, with decorative elements from *Adobe Wood Type Ornaments*.

To order additional copies of this book see the form at the back of this book or go to www.itascabooks.com

DEDICATION

THIS WORK IS DEDICATED to those who have come before us and those who will follow. Our past, present, and future are interwoven in this family tapestry.

ACKNOWLEDGMENTS

I WOULD LIKE TO THANK my husband, Mark, and my children, Matthew and Megan, for their patience and support. I would like to honor my parents for their love and encouragement. Much thanks goes to Pam Price for her meticulous editing. The staff of Mighty Media deserves credit for their careful work. But I would especially like to thank Viola Terrazas, Maria Muñoz, Celia Diaz, and Lupe Urias for sharing their lives and stories with me. This work wouldn't have been possible without them.

Contents

DESCENDANTS OF MIGUEL TERRAZAS

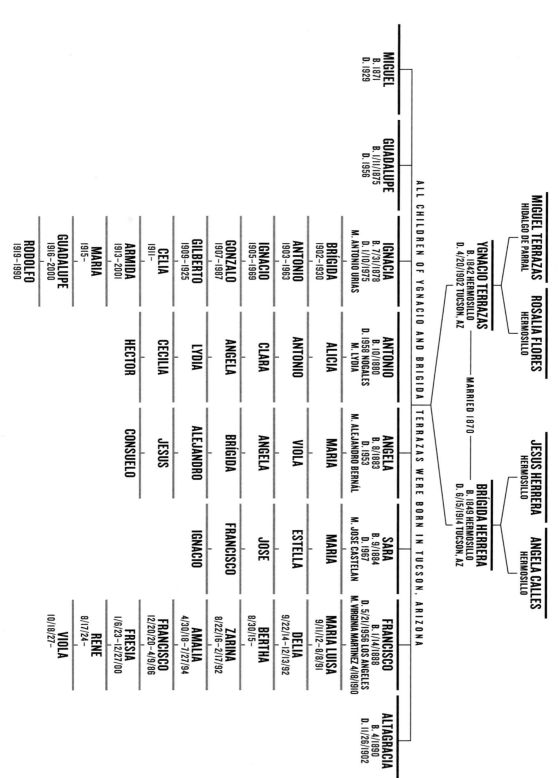

MIGUEL
B. 1871
D. 1929

GUADALUPE
B. 1/11/1875
D. 1956

MIGUEL TERRAZAS
HIDALGO DE PARRAL

ROSALIA FLORES
HERMOSILLO

YGNACIO TERRAZAS
B. 1842 HERMOSILLO
D. 4/20/1902 TUCSON, AZ

——— MARRIED 1870 ———

JESUS HERRERA
HERMOSILLO

ANGELA CALLES
HERMOSILLO

BRÍGIDA HERRERA
B. 1849 HERMOSILLO
D. 6/15/1914 TUCSON, AZ

ALL CHILDREN OF YGNACIO AND BRIGIDA TERRAZAS WERE BORN IN TUCSON, ARIZONA

IGNACIA
B. 7/31/1878
D. 1/10/1975
M. ANTONIO URIAS

BRÍGIDA
1902-1930

ANTONIO
1903-1963

IGNACIO
1905-1969

GONZALO
1907-1987

GILBERTO
1909-1925

CELIA
1911-

ARMIDA
1913-2001

MARIA
1915-

GUADALUPE
1916-2000

RODOLFO
1919-1990

ANTONIO
B. 10/1880
D. 1958 NOGALES
M. LYDIA

ALICIA

ANTONIO

CLARA

ANGELA

LYDIA

CECILIA

HECTOR

VIOLA

ANGELA

BRÍGIDA

ALEJANDRO

JESUS

CONSUELO

ANGELA
B. 8/1883
D. 1953
M. ALEJANDRO BERNÁL

MARIA

VIOLA

ANGELA

BRÍGIDA

FRANCISCO

IGNACIO

SARA
B. 9/1884
D. 1967
M. JOSE CASTELAN

MARIA

JOSE

ESTELLA

FRANCISCO

AMALIA
4/30/18-7/27/94

ZARINA
8/22/16-2/17/92

BERTHA
8/30/15-

DELIA
9/22/14-12/13/92

MARIA LUISA
9/11/12-8/8/91

FRANCISCO
B. 1/14/1888
D. 5/21/1956 LOS ANGELES
M. VIRGINIA MARTINEZ 4/18/1910

FRANCISCO
12/20/20-4/9/86

FRESIA
1/6/23-12/27/00

RENE
8/17/24-

VIOLA
10/18/27-

ALTAGRACIA
B. 4/1890
D. 11/26/1902

DESCENDANTS OF VICENTE MARTINEZ

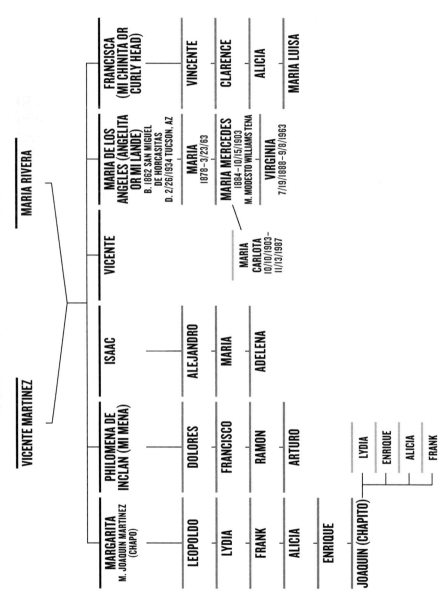

VICENTE MARTINEZ — MARIA RIVERA

MARGARITA
M. JOAQUIN MARTINEZ
(CHAPO)

PHILOMENA DE
INCLAN (MI MENA)

ISAAC

VICENTE

MARIA DE LOS
ANGELES (ANGELITA
OR MI LANDE)
B. 1862 SAN MIGUEL
DE HORCASITAS
D. 2/26/1934 TUCSON, AZ

FRANCISCA
(MI CHINITA OR
CURLY HEAD)

LEOPOLDO

DOLORES

ALEJANDRO

MARIA
1878–3/23/63

VINCENTE

LYDIA

FRANCISCO

MARIA

MARIA MERCEDES
1884–10/15/1903
M. MODESTO WILLIAMS TENA

CLARENCE

FRANK

RAMON

ADELENA

MARIA
CARLOTA
10/10/1903–
11/13/1987

VIRGINIA
7/19/1888–9/8/1963

ALICIA

ALICIA

ARTURO

MARIA LUISA

ENRIQUE

JOAQUIN (CHAPITO)

LYDIA

ENRIQUE

ALICIA

FRANK

Introduction

¡Ánimo y arriba los corazones!

WHEN I WAS A CHILD my mother entertained me with stories of her youth. Her stories were poignant memories of Tucson – the Tucson of her past. The stories revolved around childhood pranks, adventures, mysteries, and ghost stories. I loved those tales full of the history of southern Arizona.

My mother, Amalia Terrazas Goodman, was a second generation Tucsonian. Her grandparents had immigrated to Arizona from Sonora, Mexico, in 1870. Their descendants, our family, still live in Tucson. Ours is a huge extended family and we owe our heritage to those who have gone before us.

I was distraught when my mother died. I had listened to the stories of the past, but I hadn't thought it necessary to document her past. I thought she would live forever, to comfort me, to scold me, to watch my children grow.

My mother died of complications of Alzheimer's disease. Of the nine siblings in her family, five have been afflicted with Alzheimer's. Alzheimer's is a vicious disease. Not only does it debilitate the mind and body, but it also erodes the family system. It robbed me of my mother as it robbed her of her mind.

My mother's Alzheimer's disease was confirmed by autopsy. The pathologist remarked that it was most probably familial. Where does this gene come from, who was the carrier, does it matter? It does matter to me. If there is a chance that I'll become afflicted, and there surely is, I want to know that someone has collected my memories and saved them for my children.

After my mother's funeral, our family gathered to pay their respects not only to her, but to my siblings and me. This was not a sad affair. Relatives and friends brought frijoles, tamales, and tortillas. There was a steady supply of beer. As the noise level rose, people began to reminisce about my mother. Anecdotes were told, discussed, and filed away to be brought up at the next funeral.

The seed of an idea was planted in my mind that day. My cousins and I discussed the importance of documenting the Terrazas family tree. We agreed that it was something that should be done. The only thing lacking was the person willing to undertake the task.

One of my cousins, Cecilia Dicochea, had become a spokesperson of sorts. She had collected information about the Terrazas family. She was adamant about the importance of the storytelling. "We must never forget these stories," she said. "They are the priceless reminders of who we are and where we came from." Sadly enough, she died several months later of metastatic breast cancer.

The deaths of my mother and cousin were a portent that time was

Seated, left to right: Bertha T. Rodriguez, Lupe Urias, Armida U. Quiroz.
Standing, left to right: Viola Terrazas, Fresia T. Lindberg, Celia U. Diaz.

PHOTO FROM THE AUTHOR'S COLLECTION

1996

running out. I felt an urgency about recording things that I could remember. I was afraid that unless someone documented our family history soon, the wonderful stories would be lost. It was imperative to me that this not be allowed to occur.

And so I found myself returning to Tucson. I went home to visit, to pay my respects, and to try to preserve the memories of our family, the descendants of Ygnacio and Brígida Terrazas. I undertook the project as a tribute to my family and to honor their heritage.

Most of our family stories revolve around my mother's childhood home and the neighborhood it occupies. The house has been in her family for almost one hundred years and now belongs to my Aunt Viola. She is the youngest Terrazas child and has never lived anywhere but in that adobe house on South Stone Avenue. The house has been the heart and soul of our family.

The house is very ordinary, built around 1900 in Tucson. When you enter, you can clearly see that it is divided into halves. On the left, running the length of the house, are the living room, a very small bedroom, and my grandparent's room. On the right side there are a sitting room, the kitchen, and a bathroom. The wide hallway in the center serves as a dining room. On the front of the house is a porch that faces Stone Avenue. It filters out the intense light of the southern Arizona sun.

There are several family mysteries surrounding the house. It is unclear who initially owned the home. Some say that my grandmother stole the home from her mother and niece. No one knows anything about my great-grandmother or her family. There have been many rumors about her and a great deal of curiosity about both her and the original ownership of the home.

I was indeed fortunate to have the help of my extended family in this project. I was lucky to be surrounded by *tías* (aunts) who were generous in sharing their memories of our family and life in Tucson during the early 1900s. These women included my aunts Fresia, Viola, and Bertha, as well as their cousins, the Urias sisters. The two families lived within a block of one another. Although they were separate families and have their own distinct anecdotes, the stories of the two families are interwoven with a central theme of *la familia*.

This is the story of my mother and her extended family's Tucson. It was the Tucson that forever remained imprinted in their memories. It was a place they loved as they grew and changed with the city. But it became more than that to me. It is my heritage, the heritage of my huge extended family. These are our stories, the stories passed to us from our parents about the growing and changing landscape of Tucson.

CHAPTER I

Tucson ~ The Early Years

Querer y sin ganas.

TUCSON WAS ESTABLISHED by Spaniards in 1776. It served as a *presidio* (military post) for Spain until 1821 when it became a Mexican garrison. In 1853 the area south of the Gila River, including Tucson, was acquired by the United States from Mexico through the Gadsden Purchase. Between 1860 and 1880 Tucson, although a Unites States territory, was heavily influenced by the Mexican state of Sonora.

The growing number of immigrants from Mexico and other countries led to a population increase in Tucson. This expanded growth led to the incorporation of Tucson as a city in 1877. The population in 1870 was roughly 4,000 with an increase of 2,800 between 1870 and 1880. This increase was predominantly due to immigrants from Mexico.

It has often been said that the border between Arizona and Sonora, Mexico, was invisible. There was no physical boundary to prevent people from passing to one country from the next. After 1870 an exodus of poorer Mexicans from Sonora to Arizona began. It is estimated that roughly 7,500 emigrated to Arizona due to unstable conditions within Mexico, including political instability and economic exploitation. For poorer Mexicans, the policies of Porfirio Diaz, the Mexican President, generated a vast, mobile labor pool in northern Mexico. It was easy for Mexican citizens to cross the border into Arizona, lured, in part, by an expanding U.S. economy.[1]

Ygnacio Terrazas de Flores was born in 1842 in Hermosillo, Mexico. He was the son of Miguel Terrazas of Hidalgo de Parral and Rosalia Flores of Hermosillo.[2] Although not substantiated, the current members of the Terrazas family believe that Miguel Terrazas was related to the Terrazas family from the state of Chihuahua. He might have been the son of one of three brothers who emigrated from Spain to Mexico in the early 1800s. The Terrazas family acquired vast amounts of land in Chihuahua and founded one of the largest haciendas in northern Mexico. Ygnacio Terrazas married Brígida Herrera de Calles in 1870.

Brígida and Ygnacio Terrazas.   *c. 1900*
PHOTO COURTESY OF CELIA DIAZ

Little is known about Brígida's family except that her father was Jesus Herrera and her mother was Angela Calles, and that both were from Hermosillo. Brígida was born in 1849 in Hermosillo.

No one can be sure what the exact rationale was for the immigration of Ygnacio and Brígida Terrazas to Tucson. Perhaps it was the lure of a better life that beckoned them. Imagine if you will the obstacles that Ygnacio and his new bride, Brígida, had to endure in traveling from Hermosillo, Sonora, to Tucson. The distance from Hermosillo to Tucson is roughly 400 miles of harsh Sonoran desert. Not only would they have had to brave the elements, including heat, winds and dust, and a scarcity of water, they would have also had to contend with the threat of attack by hostile bands of Apache Indians.

The story that has been handed down indicates that Ygnacio and Brígida Terrazas made the journey with Jules Le Flein and his wife. The relationship between the two families is unknown, but they must have been *compadres* (close friends). Each family traveled by covered wagon.[3] Pima County census records from 1900 indicate that the Terrazas family arrived in Tucson sometime during 1870. The 1870 census, which was completed in late June of that year, does not include either the Terrazas or the Le Flein families, indicating that they probably reached Tucson late in 1870. It makes sense that their trip was probably made in the later part of the year because it would have been cooler. The temperatures of the Sonoran desert before late September would have been hazardous. Their journey probably took over a month, as wagons were notoriously slow moving; they would have been lucky to travel ten miles a day. They must have been elated upon arriving safely in Tucson.

Ygnacio Terrazas was a blacksmith by trade and Jules Le Flein was a stonemason. It may be surmised that the two men felt that their skills would enable them to find work in the growing town of Tucson. Once they arrived, Ygnacio established himself as a blacksmith by opening up a business in town. Jules was involved in the construction of St. Joseph's Academy, St. Mary's Hospital, and the original San Agustin Cathedral. He was known as *El León de Piedra* (the lion of stone) because of his skill as a master stonemason.[4] Ygnacio, skilled in surveying as well as iron work, was perhaps also involved minimally in the construction of some of these buildings as well.

The 1870s brought many changes to Tucson, primarily due to the fact that it was the territorial capital. The construction of the San Agustin Cathedral paved the way for religious educators.[5] In 1870 the Sisters of St. Joseph opened an "Academy for Young Ladies." The San Agustin Parochial School for Boys was opened in 1874. The first solvent public school was opened in 1872.[6]

Many other important events occurred in Tucson during 1873. Streets were laid out and named. The city of Tucson paid the U.S. $1,600 for town site land to be used for further construction of homes and businesses. The first grass lawns began appearing. The War Department selected a new site for Camp Lowell on the Rillito River, seven miles northeast of the city.[7] But the most important event was the arrival of the first telegraph line to Tucson. This came about because General Crook was assigned to Arizona Territory to help establish a peace policy with the Apache Indian bands (attempts to place the Apaches on reservations had intensified hostility between them and the citizens of the Territory).[8] General Crook needed a telegraph line to communicate with his staff and superiors. This line rapidly connected Tucson to the rest of the country.

In the midst of these events, the first child of Ygnacio and Brígida Terrazas was born in 1871. This child, Miguel, was the first person in the Terrazas family to be born in the United States. Ygnacio and Brígida also had two daughters during this decade. Guadalupe was born in 1875 and Ignacia was born in 1878. These were important occasions for the family. They would thereafter say that they were American of Mexican descent. This became a significant statement within the Terrazas family as recognition of their cultural heritage. They were Americans first, but their cultural background was Mexican. This was a saying that was passed on within the Terrazas family generation after generation and was something to be proud of.

The expansion of Tucson continued. Businesses were established that brought further improvements in the life of its citizens. The Eagle Steam Flour Mill was built on Main Street.[9] Paul Maroney implemented plans for bringing the first ice plant to Tucson. By 1876 the ice plant was in operation in Levine's Park.[10] When silver and copper were discovered in southeastern Arizona, Tucson was used as a commercial center to serve and supply the mining towns in the southern portion of the Territory.[11]

Mexican immigration to Tucson increased the number of unskilled laborers. Only 9 percent of Spanish-surnamed individuals held skilled positions.[12] In the 1870s, a blacksmith was considered a skilled occupation. Ygnacio Terrazas, being a blacksmith, was a skilled worker and held a respected position within the Mexican community at that time. He was well established in his business by the end of the 1870s. He had acquired property on South Stone Avenue where both his business and home were located. His shop address was listed as 362 South Stone while the residence was at 358 South Stone.[13] Ygnacio's granddaughter Celia Diaz recalled that he was socially involved within the community by that time.

The Mexican community of Tucson experienced distinct residential separation from the Anglo community. Most Mexicans lived in the *Barrio Libre* bounded by Cushing Street on the north, 18th Street on the south, and Main and Stone to the west and east. This was the original Barrio Libre district.[14] The Terrazas family became an integral part of the Mexican barrio. Both their business and their family lives revolved around this area. This was the community from which our stories have evolved.

———•••———

[1]   Sheridan, Thomas. *Los Tucsonenses* (Tucson: The University of Arizona Press, 1986), 39, 76–77.

[2]   Dicochea, Cecilia. Collected Terrazas Family History, 1980.

[3]   Celia Diaz, interview by author, 22 August 1996.

[4]   Chambers, George and Sonnichsen, C.L. *San Agustin: First Cathedral Church in Arizona* (Tucson: Arizona Historical Society and Arizona Silhouettes, 1974), 19.

[5]   Ibid., 16–17.

[6]   Sheridan, *Los Tucsonenses*, 46.

[7]   Chambers and Sonnichsen, *San Agustin*, 17; Cosulich, Bernice. *Tucson Chronology* (Tucson: Arizona Historical Society and Arizona Silhouettes, 1953), 304.

[8]   Worcester, Donald. *The Apaches: Eagles of the Southwest* (Norman, Okla.: University of Oklahoma Press, 1979), 121.

[9]   Cosulich, *Tucson Chronology*, 304.

[10] *Arizona Daily Star*, 22 July 1956.

11   Varney, Phillip. *Arizona Ghost Towns & Mining Camps* (Phoenix: Arizona Highways Book, 1994), 116; Sheridan, *Los Tucsonenses*, 86.

12   Sheridan, *Los Tucsonenses*, 87.

13   Tucson Directories, 1897–98.

14   Sheridan, *Los Tucsonenses*, 82.

CHAPTER 2

Establishing Our Terrazas Family

Lo que se siembra se recoge.

BY 1880 there were 7,007 people in Tucson – 4,469 of whom had Spanish surnames – and Tucson was becoming an important central city in the Southwest.

The Southern Pacific Railroad reached Tucson from Yuma on March 17, 1880. Tucson citizens and dignitaries turned out to welcome the railroad at an official celebration held three days later. Cannons boomed, music blared, and there were many speeches. This became one of the most important events in Tucson's history because it marked the end of the town's isolation. Tucson was now part of a rail network that extended from the east coast to the west coast. As the rail links grew, Tucson also became connected to other communities within the Territory.[1]

With the railroad came an influx of new immigrants to Tucson. Due to their work on the railroad, Tucson saw an increase in the Chinese population. Both the military and the railroad brought blacks. The mining industry drew more Europeans to the area.

The Sisters of St. Joseph realized that Tucson was in need of a hospital and opened St. Mary's Hospital on April 24, 1880.[2] St. Mary's became the most important health facility in Tucson. It was initially a community hospital, but by the mid-1880s also incorporated a tuberculosis sanitorium.

Tucson's public and private schools continued to grow. By the early 1800s roughly 230 students were enrolled in educational programs.

Brígida and Ygnacio Terrazas encouraged the education of their children. The children probably attended school through the eighth grade. Miguel Terrazas attended the Marist College, which was on Ochoa Street, and was awarded a gold cross for scholarly achievement when he graduated. Ygnacio's granddaughters assume that Miguel's brothers were also educated by the Marists. The daughters attended St. Joseph's Academy on South Sixth Avenue at 14th Street.[3]

The Terrazas family continued to expand. Four children were born during the 1880s. They included Antonio (10/80), Angela (8/83), Sara (9/84), and Francisco (1/88). By 1889, Brígida and Ygnacio Terrazas had seven children and were well established within the community. Their daughter Ignacia recalled that her family life in Tucson was relaxed and gay and quiet but not dull.[4]

Ygnacio, described as an astute businessman, began acquiring property around Tucson during the late 1880s. According to Celia Diaz (Ygnacio's granddaughter), Ygnacio owned four buildings on one block of South Stone Avenue. (This information is confirmed by the 1880 census). One was a home, one was his business, and the other two were probably rental properties. Celia recalls them as being long, low, white structures that were built of adobe.

By the early 1880s hotels and resorts were being established. One, Silver Lake swimming bath, was opened in 1881. It was a popular resort located at the base of A Mountain, west of Tucson. Tucson hosted various military dignities at its new hotels. On April 10, 1882, General William Tecumseh Sherman visited Tucson. In 1883 a reception was given in Tucson for General George Crook and his staff.[5]

From 1882 through 1886 General Crook returned to Arizona to reestablish peaceful relations with the Apache. The peace he had negotiated earlier had disintegrated and several bands of Apaches had left the San Carlos Reservation and raided throughout southern Arizona and northern Mexico. General Nelson Miles relieved Crook in 1886 and was given orders to capture or destroy the hostile bands.

After many military forays and much fear by citizens in the Territory, Geronimo finally surrendered to First Lieutenant Charles Gatewood. He was then taken and formally surrendered to General Miles on Sept. 4, 1886. Four days later Geronimo and fourteen of his warriors were sent to Fort Pickens, Florida, to be imprisoned.[6]

The citizens of Arizona Territory gave a sigh of relief; the citizens of Tucson were especially thankful. On November 8, 1887, Tucsonans presented a gold sword to General Miles in appreciation of having "ended the Apache threat." A parade was held with representatives from all the social organizations in the town. The 4th U.S. Cavalry, the Zeckendorf band, and school children with their teachers marched in the parade. The *Tucson Daily Star* noted that "400 Papagoes dressed in war paint and feathers either rode on horseback or marched in the procession." The whole town turned out to witness the military parade.[7]

Many years later, the event was described by Ignacia Terrazas Urias. The Terrazas family had participated in the event with the other citizens of Tucson, and Ignacia remembered being in the crowd that lined both sides of Meyer Street. She would have been eight years old at the time. Although she recalled it as a parade to witness the capture of Geronimo, he was in no way involved. What she actually saw was the Papago procession. At any rate, it was an occasion that remained in Ignacia's memory for many years.[8]

In 1885 the Territorial Legislature, which had convened in Prescott, appropriated $25,000 to start the University of Arizona. In 1886 the first Board of Regents of the University of Arizona met and accepted 40 acres of land given by Tucson gamblers.[9] It was located roughly one mile east of town and ground was broken for the first building in 1887. The University of Arizona was under construction even before the first public high school was established. It was a source of great pride for the Territory.

In 1886, influenced by his studies of the Woodward garden in San Francisco, Leopoldo Carillo constructed a garden for the city of Tucson. The area he developed, El Ojitos, was west of South Main on Mission Road. (Mission Road was an extension of Simpson.) Señor Carillo developed a series of pools at the south end of the garden. These pools were cemented on one side and used for carp ponds. In the largest pool, at the extreme south, he built a tiny island. The pools were fed by the natural springs found in El Ojitos, a series of which ran under the grounds. Señor Carillo brought plants and vines from San Francisco. Rows of ash, mulberry, and other trees surrounded these small lakes.[10] There were also rose bushes, flowering shrubs, and grape vines. This area came to be known as Carillo Gardens.

Carillo Gardens was a gift to the citizens of Tucson and was greatly enjoyed. An oasis in the desert, it provided refreshing baths, a dance pavilion, rowboats, and a menagerie. Every 15 minutes an express wagon carried people from locations on Main, Congress, and Meyer to the Gardens.[11] The Gardens, as it came to be called, was a major source of entertainment for the citizens of the town. It was also a source of pride as there was nothing else like it in the Southwest at the time.

Francisco Terrazas' children recalled that he delighted them with his stories about his family's outings to Carillo Gardens. The whole Terrazas family would make a day of it, complete with a picnic lunch. The children would play by the water, the adults would relax in the shade of the trees, and everyone would enjoy the flowers.

The 1890s continued to bring many changes to Tucson. Although it was a southwestern town with deep ties to the Mexican community, the majority of control was with Anglo citizens.[12] The Mexican barrios were well defined and located south of Congress and west of Stone Avenue. Anglo neighborhoods were north of Congress and extended toward the University of Arizona.

The Terrazas family lived and conducted business within the close-knit Mexican community. Although the children had been educated and could speak English, Spanish was their primary language. They were taught to be polite and answer questions when asked. They were encouraged to stay within the Mexican community and interact with Anglos only in a school or business setting. These were mores that were handed down to their children as well.

The Terrazas family was bilingual. Francisco Terrazas felt that the family could keep their cultural identity by speaking Spanish within their community. When interacting with the Anglo community, they were expected to speak English. This became a crucial theme not only for the Terrazas family, but also for the majority of Mexican-American families living in Tucson at that time. They continued to maintain their cultural identity with Mexico. However, they considered themselves Americans of Mexican descent. This belief was handed down to the following generations and was something to be proud of. When called culturally based names, the Terrazas descendants have always responded with that saying, "We are Americans of Mexican descent. We have been in this country since the 1800s; we are as American as anyone else.

We have kept our culture and traditions and we are very proud of that."

The atmosphere of the city was changing and it was becoming "more civilized." In 1891 the War Department ordered that Fort Lowell be closed. With the Apache threat eliminated, there was no longer the need for military involvement around Tucson. The University of Arizona opened its doors for the first students that same year. There was a great sense of pride connected with the university, not only for citizens of Tucson, but also for the citizens of the Arizona Territory.

As the population of Tucson grew, it was decided that the original San Agustin Cathedral was becoming too small for its expanding congregation. In 1893 construction of a new cathedral was started. It was completed by 1898 and called the Saint Augustine Cathedral. I assume that the name San Agustin was changed to Saint Augustine due to the changing population of Tucson at the time. Not only was the name updated, but it reflected the influence of the Anglo politicians and religious leaders in the city. The cathedral was located on South Stone Avenue between West Ochoa and West Corral streets. It was of modified Spanish design with double towers and a red tile roof. The location of the new cathedral was very convenient for the Terrazas family. It was only several short blocks from their home. Much of their family life revolved around religious activities.

By now, the family of Brígida and Ygnacio Terrazas was well entrenched in the community. Miguel, Guadalupe, and Ignacia were young adults, while Antonio, Angela, Sara, and Francisco were adolescents. The youngest child, Altagracia, was born in 1890. The Tucson Directories, which began publication during the 1880s, list the family's home and business addresses. The Terrazas family is also listed in the 1890 census.

Ygnacio Terrazas' dream was to find a mine. He spent much of his free time in the desert searching for a mining bonanza. His weekends and holidays were spent roaming canyons looking for a lode similar to those found around Tombstone. His weekdays were spent at his blacksmith shop. He had more than enough work and was able to include his eldest son, Miguel, in the business. At some point during the late 1890s Ygnacio began acquiring rental properties in Tucson. The rent from these homes supplemented the family income. It was another sign of his success within the business community.

Brígida Terrazas devoted all her time to raising her children. It was an enormous job to raise eight children. However, as was typical of large families during this time, the older children were required to help in the household tasks. Brígida spent much of her time cooking, cleaning, and making clothes for the children. It is interesting to note that although his granddaughters can recall anecdotal stories about Ygnacio, there are no family stories about Brígida.

Miguel was now a young man. He continued to live at home and followed in his father's footsteps. The 1880 census indicated that he was a blacksmith, employed in his father's shop. Miguel is somewhat of a mystery to his family. Many stories have been told about him. When he had finished school, the Marist priests wanted his parents to send him to Santa Fe to study for the priesthood. He very much wanted to do this, but his parents refused because they couldn't bear to be parted from him. This was devastating for him and a short time later he became ill. It is unclear what sort of illness he had, but he was sent to a small town in Sonora to recuperate. When he returned he became an apprentice to his father. What is known was that he was quite unhappy after his return to Tucson.[13]

The Terrazas children had a very strict upbringing, but it was a loving household. The family enjoyed entertaining close friends and often had dances and sang songs. Brígida served refreshments, as was the custom. The popular dances at the time were the chotis, mazurka, polkas, and danzas. They made trips to Magdalena, Sonora, for the feast day of San Francisco. They visited San Xavier Mission south of Tucson and had picnics on the banks of the Santa Cruz River.[14] Family outings to Carrillo Gardens were a favorite of the children.

The first Terrazas children were now entering young adulthood. As was the custom of Mexican families during this era, they lived at home until they married. The young ladies were closely chaperoned by older aunts, cousins, or family friends. They were never to be in the company of a young man unless a chaperone was with them. This custom was never questioned and Ygnacio was very firm about it. His granddaughters can still remember stories of Ignacia entertaining friends at home, especially her novio, Antonio Urias. The young adults would sit in the front room of the home and play music and sing. At 9 P.M. Ygnacio would announce to the group that it was time for them to go home. He was very stern and this caused a bit of an embarrassment for his daughter Ignacia.[15]

The Terrazas children looked forward to the new century. 1900 was rung in with much revelry. Families gathered, and at the stroke of midnight noisy celebrations could be heard. Church bells were rung, horns and whistles were blown, and guns were fired. The arrival of the new century heralded many changes for the city of Tucson. Many changes were in store for the Terrazas family as well.

The population of Tucson in 1900 was 7,531 with almost 55 percent being Mexican-American. Of the Spanish-surnamed residents, 99 percent had either been born in the United States or in north-central Mexico. This made Tucson an ethnic enclave. Mexican-Americans were able to move through the blue-collar ranks, but few were able to get into better-paying white-collar jobs. Mexican-Americans became proprietors, peddlers, vendors, seamstresses, and carpenters while there were few government officials, bankers, or accountants.[16] Tucson continued to be largely controlled by the Anglo minority.

Life was a struggle for these people. To bring meaning to life they created a society for themselves, building a culture rooted in the Tucson barrios.[17] They had their own newspaper, *El Fronterizo*. They had their own religious and patriotic celebrations. The *Alianza Hispano-Americana* was a civic organization formed to promote and protect their culture. Ygnacio Terrazas was a member of this group.[18] They listened to their own music and musicians. They attended Mexican theaters, circuses, and vaudeville performances. These things helped the Mexican-American population preserve and continue their cultural traditions.

Meanwhile, the Anglo-controlled government proceeded to make changes within Tucson. Military Plaza, which occupied roughly twenty-three acres, had become vacant. This land was divided and eventually became the sites for the Carnegie Library, the Santa Rita Hotel, and Armory Park.[19]

Ygnacio Terrazas continued his searches for veins of ore. Sometime in late 1901 he became lost on one of his excursions. This was quite unusual as he was very familiar with the desert surrounding Tucson. It was believed by his children that he suffered a stroke. Somehow, he managed to wander back to town, but he was never the same and was unable to work. Around this time the family had moved to a home at

418 South Convent, home of Brígida and Ygnacio Terrazas. *c. 1960*
PHOTO COURTESY OF VIOLA TERRAZAS

418 South Convent.[20] The home and business on South Stone Avenue were never mentioned again in the Tucson Directory. Ygnacio died on April 20, 1902.[21] He was buried in the community cemetery, which was located at Speedway and Stone.

Before Ygnacio died, two of his children had married. Ignacia married Antonio Urias on November 8, 1900, and Antonio married Lydia Flynn on April 12, 1902.[22] This is important because the properties that Ygnacio owned were divided between his unmarried children. These properties were 418 South Convent, 621 South 3rd Avenue, and 622 South Bean Avenue. Brígida and her remaining children continued to live in the property at 418 South Convent. It was believed by family members that the property on South Stone Avenue was sold and the property on Convent was purchased from those proceeds.

Another tragedy befell the family in that same year. Altagracia Terrazas had occupied a special position within the family as the youngest member. While climbing in a large fig tree behind the family home, she suffered a serious fall. She sustained a severe head injury and died on

November 26, 1902. The stress of losing both her husband and youngest child greatly affected Brígida. She was overcome with sorrow and never completely recovered from these events.

As was the custom, both newly married couples lived close to their families. Antonio and Ignacia Urias lived at 135 West Cushing Street. Antonio and Lydia Terrazas lived at 153 South Convent. Both Antonio and Ignacia provided emotional and probably financial support to Brígida.

After 1902 Miguel continued to be listed in the Tucson Directories and shared the same residence with his mother. However, neither an occupation nor a business address is listed for him. This leads one to conclude that either the death of his father or some other emotional insult prevented Miguel from ever working again. At this point he became dependent on his family for financial support.

Guadalupe Terrazas, also known as Lupita, also continued to live with her mother. She helped her mother with the everyday tasks of cooking, cleaning, and sewing for her siblings. Although Guadalupe was not considered unattractive, she had suffered from either smallpox or acne and had a very scarred face. She was very self-conscious about this and as a result was very shy and withdrawn. She would remain a *soltera* (old-maid).

Although the exact dates are unknown, both Angela and Sara Terrazas also married sometime during the decade of 1900. Angela married Alejandro Bernal and shortly afterward they moved to Los Angeles, California. Sara married Jose Castelan and they moved to Nogales, Arizona.

The men in this family found employment in white-collar jobs. Antonio Terrazas was employed by the Tucson Grocery Company as a salesman. Antonio Urias was employed by Zeckendorf's as a traveling salesman selling dry goods in Mexico. Francisco Terrazas worked for the Southern Pacific Railroad as a laborer in the roundhouse. Since Francisco was unmarried at this time, he continued to live in the family home.

Because of their jobs all three men began commuting between Tucson and Nogales. Between 1903 and 1906 Antonio Terrazas decided to start his own grocery business. For some reason he moved his family to Nogales and started the business there. Francisco's job with the railroad frequently took him to Nogales and required that he spend short amounts of time there. Antonio Urias had to pass through Nogales on his travels into Mexico. He often spent time with his brother-in-law Antonio Terrazas and his family.

When business took him to Nogales, Francisco Terrazas ate meals at a boarding house owned and operated by Maria de Los Angeles Martinez. She had three daughters who helped her run her business. While there, Francisco met one of her daughters, Virginia Martinez. They were married in 1910 in Tucson. Francisco then went to work as a clerk for the Pacific Grocery store. He and Virginia moved into the family home on 418 South Convent.

The information available on Virginia Martinez and her family is very sketchy. Death certificates have been verified on her family members in the state of Arizona, but little is known about the family when they lived in Mexico. Information from relatives and death certificates has confirmed that the Martinez family was originally from San Miguel de Horcasitas, Sonora.

Virginia's mother, Maria de Los Angeles Martinez, was born in 1862 in San Miguel de Horcasitas, Mexico. Her parents were Vicente Martinez and Maria Rivera. Maria de Los Angeles was called Angelita, but her nickname was Mi Lande. She was the fifth of six children. Nothing is known about her life before she moved to Nogales, Arizona.

The family history surrounding her is fairly obscure. It is believed that she was widowed and following the death of her husband she opened a boarding house in Nogales. Around the turn of the century, the owning and operating of a boarding house was considered a reputable business for a woman who had to support herself and her children. Angelita had three daughters, Maria (1878), Maria Mercedes (1884), and Virginia (1888).

The family was lead to believe that both Maria and Maria Mercedes were half-sisters to Virginia. No information is known about their father (or fathers). Maria was much darker complected and not as attractive as her two sisters. As a result, she was treated differently than they were and in later years was ostracized by her family.

Angelita's second daughter, Maria Mercedes, was said to be beautiful. She married Modesto Williams, a British railroad engineer. Modesto had been orphaned at an early age and was raised by Mexican

Maria Mercedes and Virginia Martinez.   *c. 1900*

PHOTO COURTESY OF VIOLA TERRAZAS

Courtesy of the Arizona Historical Society/Tucson. 91655

foster parents. They renamed him Modesto Williams Tena when he was baptized. He was burned and subsequently died in 1904 following a railroad accident in Mexico.[23]

Maria Mercedes and Modesto Tena had a child who was born on October 10, 1903. Her name was Maria Carlota Tena. It was a difficult labor and delivery and Maria Mercedes died five days later. Her mother, Angelita Martinez, raised Maria Carlota. This child was told that Angelita was her mother, but at age ten learned the true circumstances of her birth. It was a complete shock to her to learn that the woman she had regarded as her mother was in fact her grandmother. Upon the death of her father Carlota Tena received a substantial railroad pension, which was held in trust for her by her grandmother.[24] In the ensuing years Angelita's remaining two daughters married men from Tucson. Virginia married Francisco Terrazas and Maria married Apolonio Cienfuegos. These two daughters then moved to Tucson. For a time Angelita continued to run her boarding house in Nogales. In 1917 she sold the boarding house and she and Carlota moved to Tucson. Angelita used the money from Carlota's trust to buy a home in Tucson. This home was located at 591 South Stone Avenue and is still in the hands of Angelita's grandchildren.

———•••———

1   Haney, John and Scavone, Cirino. "Cars Stop Here" *Smoke Signal* 23 (1971) 47; Sheridan, *Los Tucsonenses*, 55.

2   Cosulich, *Tucson Chronology*, 304.

3   Maria Muñoz, interview by author, 3 May 1997.

4   *Arizona Daily Star*, 4 April 1971.

5   Cosulich, *Tucson Chronology*, 304.

6   Lockwood, Frank. *The Apache Indians* (Lincoln, Neb.: University of Nebraska Press, 1987), 291, 300.

7   *Tucson Daily Star*, 9 November 1887.

8   *Arizona Daily Star*, 4 April 1971.

9   Cosulich, *Tucson Chronology*, 305.

10   *Arizona Daily Star*, 12 May 1886.

11   Ibid.

12   Sheridan, *Los Tucsonenses*, 56.

13   Muñoz interview, 1997.

14   *Arizona Daily Star*, 4 April 1971.

15   Muñoz interview, 1997.

16   Sheridan, *Los Tucsonenses*, 126, 129.

17   Ibid., 130.

18   Celia Diaz, interview by author, 22 August 1996.

19   Sheridan, *Los Tucsonenses*, 124.

20   Tucson Directory, 1902.

21   Death Register of St. Augustine's Cathedral, vol. 2, 117.

22   Marriage Register of St. Augustine's Cathedral.

23   Dicochea, Family History, 1980.

24   Ibid.

CHAPTER 3

The Second Generation

No más entran como burros sin mecate.

THE TERRAZAS FAMILY was now fairly large and four of the siblings had remained in Tucson. Miguel and Guadalupe were to remain unmarried. The following chapters involve only the families of Antonio and Ignacia Urias and Francisco and Virginia Terrazas. Although Ignacia and Francisco kept in close contact with their other siblings, these two became particularly close. Their family lives were intertwined. As their families grew, they shared their trials and tribulations. It is their memories of growing up in Tucson during the early 1900s that are shared here. Not only did they grow up in the city, but they also watched the city expand and change around them. These are our family stories.

From 1882 until the early part of the 1900s Territorial Legislators lobbied Congress to admit Arizona to the Union. It was a long and difficult battle. Their efforts were finally rewarded on February 14, 1912, when Arizona became the 48th state. The Terrazas family often called it the "baby state" because, in their time, it was the last state admitted to the Union. They were quite proud that their native home had gained statehood.

Ignacia Terrazas Urias and her husband, Antonio, had now started their large family. Their first five children were born in the first decade of the 1900s. They included Brígida (6/21/02), Antonio (10/12/03), Ignacio (9/14/05), Gonzalo (6/29/07), and Gilberto (4/3/09). Celia (5/11/11), Armida (6/3/13), Maria (1/23/15), Guadalupe (7/3/16), and Rodolfo (5/10/19) were born during the second decade of the 1900s.

Antonio Urias was descended from a family that had lived in Tucson since the early 1800s. He met Ignacia Terrazas when they were in school. Antonio attended the Marist College and Ignacia attended the St. Joseph School. Antonio frequently walked Ignacia home from school. When he courted Ignacia, he rented a *berlina* (horse-drawn carriage) and took her to Carillo Gardens. He also called on her at her home. A chaperone was always present during these meetings. When they were in the Terrazas home, Ignacia's father would always announce that Antonio had to leave at 9 P.M.[1]

Antonio Urias married Ignacia Terrazas at St. Augustine Cathedral on November 8,1900. He had a very respectable job as a salesman for Zeckendorf's mercantile from 1891 until 1916. He and Ignacia initially lived at 135 West Cushing Street. Their first nine children were born in that home. As the family grew, a larger home was needed, and in 1917 the family moved to a home at 720 South Sixth Avenue.[2]

In 1916, Antonio began working for the Haymon Krupp Company of El Paso, Texas. As he had when he worked for Zeckendorf's, he worked as a traveling salesman selling goods in Mexico. He primarily worked in the northwestern states of Mexico, which included Sonora, Sinaloa, and Nayarit. Antonio sold mostly fabrics, bed linens, and other household items. He took orders from stores in Mexico and the Hayman Krupp Company would ship these orders to the stores. He was usually away from home for six weeks at a time. He would be back in Tucson for two weeks, and was then off again to Mexico.[3]

As Antonio Urias prospered as a salesman, he was able to purchase a very nice home for his family. It was built of red brick and had a lovely front porch supported by wooden columns. The house had three large bedrooms and a screened porch on the back. The lot had been well landscaped and had a nice lawn. There were chinaberry trees between the sidewalk and curb. In the back of the house there was a large, beautifully shaped fruitless mulberry tree. Along the south side of the house, beneath the kitchen window, were three velvety red rose bushes. Among other plants were violets, China lilies, chrysanthemums, honeysuckle, baby-rose climber, oleander, and lilacs. Ignacia loved flowers and gardening was a hobby and a way to relax.[4] The lot was unusually shaped and faced both Stone Avenue and Sixth Avenue. These were very important streets at the time because they were the primary roads out of town. The home was on the border of the Anglo neighborhoods and definitely indicated a move out of the traditional Mexican-American barrio.

Little is known of the courtship of Francisco Terrazas and Virginia Martinez. Francisco was taken with Virginia because she was fairly attractive. Virginia was impressed with what she believed was Francisco's social standing within the Mexican-American community of Tucson. She thought he was a better class of person from a very respectable family. Francisco and Virginia were married in Tucson on April 7, 1910. They lived with Brígida Terrazas at the family home on 418 South Convent. Francisco Terrazas left his job with the railroad and

Francisco Herrera Terrazas.   *c. 1900*
PHOTO COURTESY OF ARIZONA HISTORICAL SOCIETY, TUCSON
Courtesy of the Arizona Historical Society/Tucson. 91651

went to work as a clerk for the Pacific Grocery, which was located at 46 West Congress.[5]

Francisco and Virginia Terrazas had nine children. Their first child, Maria Luisa, was born on September 11, 1912. They were quite proud that she was born in the same year that Arizona acquired statehood. Maria Luisa was followed by Delia (9/22/14), Bertha (8/30/15), Zarina (8/22/16), Amalia (4/30/18), and Francisco (12/20/20). These children were born while the family lived on Convent. After the family moved to South Stone Avenue, Fresia (1/6/23), Rene (8/17/24), and Maria Linda Viola (10/18/27) were born.

Around 1912, as Francisco and Virginia's family began to expand, Brígida and her two unmarried children, Miguel and Lupe, moved from the house on South Convent to a house at 145 West Kennedy. Brígida died June 15, 1914, of pneumonia. No mention was ever again made of the house on Kennedy. Antonio and Ignacia Urias took Miguel and Lupe into their home. It is unclear why they went to live with the Urias family. Perhaps it was because Ignacia was the eldest married daughter or perhaps it was because they did not get along with Virginia. What was certain was that at this point Miguel was unable to care for himself.

The Terrazas home at 418 South Convent was typical of the houses in the Mexican-American barrio. It was built of traditional thick-walled adobe and was whitewashed. It is a long, narrow house that sits close to the street. The home contains three bedrooms. A small fireplace in the living room initially provided warmth for the home. The side and back yards were fenced for privacy – and perhaps because it is on a corner. In the back of the house were large fig trees. The home is still standing and is in the historic barrio section of Tucson.

According to family tradition, the property of Ygnacio and Brígida Terrazas would have gone to their unmarried children, Miguel and Lupe. Yet, Francisco and Virginia lived there until 1922. Why they moved is a mystery. Perhaps they were asked to move by Miguel and his sister, perhaps there was a family disagreement, or perhaps Virginia felt more comfortable living with her family. It was fairly common knowledge that the Terrazas siblings did not like Virginia. They found her to be a very domineering, aggressive woman and they felt she hen-pecked Francisco.[6]

Sometime around 1915 Francisco Terrazas went into business with

Rafael Corral and they opened the Terrazas and Corral Grocery at 199 South Convent. This store was located in the Mexican-American neighborhood of Tucson. They sold canned goods, fresh fruits and vegetables (often supplied by Antonio Terrazas from Nogales), some dairy products, and meat. They had a delivery service and goods were delivered by buckboard. In 1923 the partnership was dissolved and Francisco opened his own store, Terrazas Grocery, at 273 South Convent. The store carried the same products and he continued to offer delivery service.

In 1918 Angelita Martinez moved from Nogales to Tucson to be closer to her two married daughters, Virginia Terrazas and Maria Cienfuegos. She purchased a home at 591 South Stone Avenue from a man named Leonardo Moreno. It was to become known as the Terrazas home and is still occupied by a member of the Francisco Terrazas family.

Our family has always wondered about the home on South Stone Avenue and its origins. Uncovering the history of the house was very

Terrazas and Corral Grocery.   *1915*

PHOTO COURTESY OF ARIZONA HISTORICAL SOCIETY, TUCSON
Courtesy of the Arizona Historical Society/Tucson. B109329

important to me. Aunt Viola had the original deeds to the home and I was able to determine the identity of the original owner. The home occupies a large lot and was initially owned by Robert M. Crandal. He purchased it September 1, 1873, for $4. The deed to the property lists it as being Lot 5, Block Number 239. In 1870 Tucson was incorporated as a town, lots were surveyed, and most were sold from $5 to $10. This lot would have been one of the southernmost to be sold at the time. It was held by the Crandal family and remained vacant for quite some time. I was quite interested in who this family was and if they were in any way related to the Terrazas family.

Robert M. Crandal was born in Ohio about 1832. He grew up and went to school in Indiana. In 1852 he crossed the plains to California where he owned and operated the American Hotel in Jackson, California. During the Civil War Robert joined the 1st California Infantry where he was appointed Second Lieutenant. In 1862 Company G of the 1st California Infantry was sent to Arizona. Robert Crandal was appointed as Provost Marshal, Western District of Arizona, with headquarters at Tucson. He served in both Arizona and New Mexico during the Civil War, was promoted to Captain, and was mustered out of the service August 31, 1864.[7]

After the war, Crandal returned to Indiana following the death of his father. He had not been included in the distribution of the estate and wandered back to the Southwest. While in El Paso visiting W. W. Mills, who was the Collector of Customs, he mentioned that he was destitute and had no job prospects. Mills offered Crandal an appointment as Deputy Collector of Customs for Tucson, which he accepted. The position paid an annual salary of $1,800. Robert Crandal was officially appointed as the Mounted Inspector of Customs on December 23, 1867. He was assigned a territory west to Yuma and south to Tubac. Crandal also served as a member of the 5th Arizona Legislature, representing Pima County in 1868.[8] In 1869 he bought an interest in the La Paz silver mine, which was located roughly 12 miles west of Tucson.[9]

Robert Crandal was known as a very handsome man and described as being strong mentally and physically. In the 1870 census he was still listed as Inspector of Customs with property valued at $30,000, which was quite significant for a citizen of Tucson. Sometime before 1870 he took Griselda P. Saenz as his common-law wife. Griselda was born in

Sonora about 1838 and was listed in the 1870 census as a seamstress. They had two children, Maria (also called Mary) and Robert J. Crandal. The Crandals occupied a home that faced Church Plaza. It seems that in the early 1870s Crandal resigned his position as Inspector of Customs. He then made his livelihood as a gambler. He died in Tucson on March 2, 1876. The cause of his untimely death is unknown.[10]

Robert Crandal's will left his estate to Griselda Saenz for the support of their daughter, Mary, who was three. Griselda was pregnant with their son at the time of Robert's death and thus that child was not mentioned in the will. Crandal's estate at the time of his death was appraised at $3,945. Crandal had gambled much of his estate away. What remained included three lots, two of which were on Church Plaza and the other on Stone Avenue.[11]

Griselda probably moved to the property on 591 South Stone Avenue in 1893. Property records indicate that the house was built that year.[12] The Crandal family is not listed in the Tucson Directories until 1906–07. Then there is a listing for Mrs. Maria Crandall (note that the spelling is different). From 1906 to 1914 the Directories indicate that Mrs. Griselda Crandal, widow of Robert, lived at the address on Stone Avenue.

The house was built of adobe and originally had two large rooms in front and a sleeping porch across the back. There was also a large front porch. Because of the heat, the cooking was done in a small structure behind the house. The house was a small structure, not much room was necessary for Griselda and her son, Robert. By this time her daughter, Mary, had married and moved to New York City, so nothing larger was needed.

Griselda P. Saenz died in 1917. Maria Morrison Godfrey (whose maiden name was Mary Crandall) quitclaimed the property at 591 South Stone Avenue to her brother, Robert J. Crandall (note that the spelling is now different) on May 25, 1917. On Aug. 17, 1917, Robert J. Crandall sold the property to Leonardo Moreno for $10. In turn, Leonardo Moreno sold the property to Maria de Los Angeles Martinez (Angelita Martinez) in 1918.

This was how the property at 591 South Stone Avenue came to be known as the "Terrazas home." Angelita Martinez originally purchased the lot with money from the trust of her granddaughter, Carlota Tena.

She bought the home in Tucson to be closer to her married daughters. Initially, Virginia and Francisco Terrazas lived at 418 South Convent. Tucson Directories do not indicate that the Francisco Terrazas family moved to that address until 1922. From 1918 through 1921, the Directories indicate that only Angelita Martinez lived on Stone Avenue.

My mother, Amalia Terrazas Goodman, often said that she had been born in the house on Stone Avenue. She said that her grandmother brought her into the world. This was one of the mysteries for me in writing this work. I had assumed that all of the Terrazas children were born in the house on Stone Avenue. However, going through the old Tucson Directories, I was surprised to find that the family had not moved in with Angelita Martinez until four years after my mother's birth. I must now believe that if my mother was born in that house, it was probably because Virginia Terrazas had gone there to be attended by her mother during her labor and delivery.

What I am now writing is strictly conjecture based upon information given to me by my mother's Urias cousins and from my mother's stories. Miguel and Lupe Terrazas were left properties from their parents' estate. These properties were to go to the unmarried children. Once Brígida Terrazas died, Ignacia Urias and her family took in Miguel and Lupe. In the meantime, Miguel and Lupe allowed Francisco and his family to occupy the home on Convent Avenue.

Virginia Terrazas was a very aggressive and assertive woman, and it was she who controlled her family. These were not admirable traits in women at the time. Such women were fairly bright and their outspokenness was not well received. It was therefore not surprising that she was not well liked by her husband's siblings. The home on Convent Avenue was larger than the home on Stone Avenue. I speculate that Virginia might have done something to offend Miguel and Lupe Terrazas. At this point Francisco Terrazas and his family were asked to leave the home and had to move in with Virginia's mother. Thereafter, the home on Convent became a rental property and supported both Lupe and Miguel Terrazas.

At the time the Terrazas family moved in with Angelita Martinez they had six children. Angelita's granddaughter, Carlota Tena, also lived with her. The home on Stone Avenue was much too small for a family of this size so it was enlarged. The sleeping porch was converted into a kitchen and small bedroom, and a large master bedroom, a bathroom, and a storage area were added. There was also a screened porch added to the rear of the house, which was used as a sleeping porch for the children in the hot months of the year.

The lot on South Stone Avenue is fairly large and rectangular shaped. It measures roughly 65 feet wide and 154 feet long. The home is at the front part of the lot. I have been told, and can vaguely remember, that there was a small shack at the very back of the lot. When my mother was young this one-room shack was rented out to an elderly man. Directly behind and to the right of the house was a long narrow building constructed of adobe. The outside of this building was not plastered and whitewashed as the house was. It was plain dirt-colored adobe with a corrugated tin roof. The inside of the building was divided into three rooms and had a linoleum floor. It was a very primitive building and became the home of Angelita's daughter Maria, who was married to Apolonio Cienfuegos.

Angelita Martinez must have been a kind, generous woman. Not only did her two daughters and granddaughter share her home, but it also was not uncommon for her to take in other relatives. For a time her nephew Joaquin Martinez left his four children with her while he worked in California. Maria and Apolonio were childless and these children lived in their dwelling. Maria was devastated that she could not have children. Her husband adored her and to help her get over her loss allowed Joaquin Martinez's children to live with them. One child in particular was with them for quite some time; Alicia Martinez became a daughter to them and Apolonio paid for her education.

Unlike the Urias home, which was a block away, there was no lawn surrounding this home. In front of the sidewalk and by the street are two pepper trees. The large, gnarled oleander tree is on the left side of the front walk and an oleander shrub is to the right. The left border of the lot was lined with a pepper tree, two pomegranate bushes, and two fruitless mulberry trees. Six large oleander bushes marked the lot-line on the right. Directly behind the house was a huge canopied fig tree. It separated the main home from the small bungalow occupied by Apolonio and Maria Cienfuegos.

The Martinez/Terrazas home was on the east side of South Stone Avenue. Like the Urias home, this was a new section of Tucson and was considered to be a good neighborhood. Directly south of the home was a vacant lot, which bordered 17th Street. The Urias Family lived one block south. I am not sure if this move for the Terrazas family would have been considered a lateral or an upward move socially. Stone Avenue was a dividing line between the old barrio and the new neighborhoods of Tucson. However, they were sharing the home with Angelita Martinez. I have never heard anyone mention that this was a burden for Angelita. Over the years, the house simply came to be known as Virginia's house. It was made quite clear that Francisco Terrazas was in no way an owner of the property.

———•••———

1 Holder, Lynn. *Our Pioneer Family: Urias-Wright* (Tucson, May 1992), 85.
2 Ibid.
3 Muñoz interview, 3 May 1997.
4 Ibid.
5 Tucson Directories, 1910.
6 Muñoz interview, 1997.
7 Arizona Historical Society, Hayden Biographical file for Robert M. Crandal 1832–1876.
8 Ibid.
9 *Tucson Arizonian*, 28 May 1869.
10 *Tucson Daily Citizen*, 4 March 1876.
11 Pima County Book of Wills, vol. 1, 52.
12 Pima County Residential Property Record Card, No. 10 117 14 234.

CHAPTER *4*

Toda La Familia

En boca cerrada no entran moscas.

$\mathcal{T}$UCSON OF THE 1920S can best be described as a growing community. With a population of 20,377, it was large enough to now be called a city. Mexican-Americans had become a minority and comprised roughly one-third of the population. However, Tucson had one of the largest and most influential Mexican-American communities in the Southwest.[1]

The people of Tucson had survived the demands of World War I. The economy of the city was based on commerce rather than industry. Streets had been paved, there were electric streetlights, and there was an electric trolley system. People were buying cars. The warm climate attracted not only tourists, but also people seeking treatment for health problems, particularly tuberculosis. Health care was becoming an important aspect of the Tucson economy.

The University of Arizona had an enrollment of one thousand students. New buildings had been added to the campus. By 1915 there was an athletic field and a football team.[2] The citizens of Tucson embraced the University for it became a major force in not only the social events, but also in the economy of the city.

There had been other changes too. Carillo Gardens, which had been a favorite picnic spot for the Terrazas family, had been closed. In 1903 Emmanuel Drachman took it over and called it Elysian Grove. It encompassed thirteen acres and included a baseball field and an entertainment pavilion. Entertainment such as vaudeville, concerts, and moving pictures took place there. The first biplane to Tucson landed there in 1910. However, the Grove began to lose money. The tributary from the Santa Cruz River that fed the El Ojito springs dried up due to the irrigation that had been done. The citizens of Tucson lost interest in the Grove. It was finally closed in 1915.[3] But it remained in the memories of the Terrazas family. My mother was told about the Grove. Even though she would never see it, she remembered stories about the "oasis in the desert."

It should be understood that the Terrazas family was not merely one family. It was a large network of individuals who were related by marriage. The members of one household were connected to the members of another household. Aunts, uncles, and cousins drifted in and out of households. Certain people were tolerated more than others. Family secrets were known to adults, and later were occasionally told to adult children. Socially unaccepted individuals were merely tolerated and took their secrets to the grave.

When Francisco and Virginia Terrazas moved to the home on South Stone in 1922 they had six children. Moving in with Angelita and Carlota meant that eight people were crowded into a small home. Angelita did most of the cooking and helped care for the children. Virginia frequently helped Francisco at the grocery store. People tended to take care of one another during those times. It was not unusual to have extended family relationships; cousins or aunts and uncles would often come and stay.

It was difficult to find information on Maria de Los Angeles Martinez. Few people who are living today can remember her. She was listed in the Tucson Directories as Angelita Martinez. Her grandchildren simply called her Mi Lande. I have heard her described as a very quiet person. She was quite small and always dressed in long black skirts. There is one remaining picture of her, which must have been taken when she was in her mid to late 20s. She appears to have been an attractive woman. She was always in the background, unobtrusively helping with the children, cooking, and cleaning. She was not one to complain. She was much loved by her grandchildren and was a buffer between them and their critical mother.

Angelita Martinez would have died when my mother was an adolescent. Today no one can remember anything about Angelita Martinez's family situation. I can remember, even as a young child, asking my mother questions about Mi Lande. My mother told me that my grand-

Maria de los Angeles Martinez.   *c. 1880*
P<small>HOTO COURTESY OF</small> V<small>IOLA</small> T<small>ERRAZAS</small>

mother had two half-sisters, Maria Martinez Cienfuegos and Maria Mercedes. But I never heard anything about Angelita Martinez's husbands.

There were some things that were not discussed with children in Hispanic families of that era. An unmarried woman with children was socially unacceptable and would have been one of those topics. It was a stigma that would have followed that person to the grave. It was simply another topic that wasn't discussed by Virginia Terrazas, and was something she probably wished to be buried with her mother.

Information that I was able to find about her indicated that her maiden name was Martinez. Family records stated that she had married a man whose name was also Martinez. I had always been suspicious of a woman with a maiden name marrying a man of the same surname. I later discovered that this was not uncommon in smaller communities of Mexico. What remains confusing to me is whether Maria and Maria Mercedes were full sisters or half-sisters.

It always led me to wonder whether Angelita Martinez had ever been married. I liked to speculate that perhaps she had been a common-law wife. When I asked my mother about this possibility, she laughed and said she didn't know. None of my mother's siblings or cousins could answer this question. They said it had always been explained to them that Angelita was a widow. It makes some sense to me that they wouldn't know the truth because they would have been too young to have been told of her marital history.

There is also the great possibility that I am completely off base with my assumption, so this information should be taken with a grain of salt. It is possible that Angelita Martinez could have been married to two different men named Martinez, and had been left a widow by both. It was very common at that time to have been widowed and left with the care of several children. It was quite acceptable for widows at that time to take in boarders, which according to family lore was what Angelita had done. A woman left with three daughters would have been at a social and economic disadvantage.

This explained a great deal to me about my grandmother, Virginia Martinez Terrazas. My grandmother was very class conscious. She married my grandfather because his family was accepted socially in Tucson. She was extremely concerned about the "class of people" with whom her children were associated. My grandmother always pushed her children to "make more of themselves." This was something I heard repeatedly as I was growing up, "You must make something of yourself."

Carlota Tena also lived with the Terrazas Family. She was their cousin and was a decade older than they. Carlota was a very pretty, bright woman. She was described as being very kind and generous to her younger cousins. She treated them as younger siblings. My mother adored her.

Carlota attended the University of Arizona, which was rare for a woman, especially a woman who was of Mexican descent. When she finished her education she married a wealthy rancher in Sonora,

Mexico. This man's name was Emilio Pompa and he had a reputation for being somewhat cruel. Carlota wasn't able to have children; she had several miscarriages. Because she couldn't produce an heir and because of increasing spousal abuse, her marriage to Emilio was annulled. At that time she returned to Tucson and to the home on South Stone Avenue. She worked for a time selling cosmetics at Steinfelds Department Store. After her grandmother's death she moved to Los Angeles.

Maria Martinez Cienfuegos and her husband, Apolonio, lived in the small bungalow behind the Martinez/Terrazas home. Maria Cienfuegos was called *Prietita* (little dark one). Apolonio worked for the Southern Pacific Railroad and was often away from home. Prietita was unable to have children and was a very lonely woman. She had five small dogs, which she treated as children. The one that is most remembered is Sambo, a black Chihuahua. Sambo was her favorite, he was coddled, and he nipped when disturbed. Because the dogs were very yippy and because there was dog hair throughout the small home, the Terrazas children did not like to spend too much time there.

As her nickname described, Prietita was a dark-complected woman. No one would have described her as attractive. I have assumed from records that she was Angelita Martinez's first child and had a different father than Maria Mercedes and Virginia. Virginia was not fond of her half-sister. She was ashamed of her because she was so dark. And I suspect that she was also ashamed of her because it reinforced the constraints of their social situation.

Prietita was subject to headaches. My mother recalled that she liked to have her head rubbed and would pay the children a nickel for the task. She also gave them a penny for any gray hair they would pluck from her head. She was also subject to bouts of depression and loneliness and would use the excuse of a headache to have her nieces and nephews visit. They also thought she was a little strange and "not quite right."

Prietita longed for children. Maria Muñoz recalled that Prietita took in her cousin Joaquin "Chapo" Martinez's daughter, Alicia. It is unclear how long Alicia lived with Maria and Apolonio Cienfuegos. Apolonio provided for her and gave her spending money. She attended school in Tucson when she lived with them. Maria Muñoz remembered this because Alicia always had more spending money than the other children. Eventually, Alicia's father returned and took her to California to be with her other siblings. Prietita was again lonely. As a good husband, Apolonio vowed to find her a child. He paid a family to adopt their young daughter. The Cienfuegos had the child for a while and then her family reclaimed her. This went on several times, with the child's family demanding more money for "the adoption." Finally, the Cienfuegos realized that this was a ploy and gave up their hopes of adopting this child.

When Angelita Martinez died in 1934 and Virginia assumed the title on the property, it was no longer comfortable for the Cienfuegos to continue to live in the bungalow. They stayed there for several years, but then moved to a different home. After that the Terrazas family rarely saw Maria Cienfuegos. She was ostracized by Virginia. She died in 1963 in the Arizona State Hospital for the insane, where she had been committed. Her death certificate listed her cause of death as dementia (now probably known as Alzheimer's Disease). I can remember this because my mother forced me to go to her wake. I was ten years old at the time and didn't know who she even was as I had never met her. It was at that time that I began to question my mother about her grandmother and her mysterious social situation. But I received no answers. Now it is only speculation and will probably remain a mystery.

While Angelita Martinez took in her extended family, the same was true of the Antonio Urias family. Not only did Miguel and Lupe Terrazas live within their home, but they too welcomed other family members in times of need. Since Antonio Urias was frequently away in Mexico on business, Ignacia ran the home. Her sister Lupe was a great help and her major tasks were cooking and helping with the laundry.

Miguel Terrazas was something of an enigma. My mother used to tell stories about him. However, I have since found that her stories were laced with misunderstanding. Maria Urias Muñoz supplied me with much of the information about Tío Miguel. Why he didn't work remains a mystery. He received money from a rental property on Bean Avenue, which had been left to him by his father. He and his sister Lupe shared the back bedroom of the Urias home. Theirs was the largest of the three bedrooms. Miguel spent most of his time in his room and Lupe would take his meals in to him.

As Maria Muñoz explained to me, Miguel was the Terrazas family's skeleton in the closet. Although Miguel was sober much of the time, he was an alcoholic. This was the era of prohibition and liquor was not easy to obtain. Because of this, Miguel drank Agua Florida, which was a cologne and naturally composed of alcohol. He usually stayed in the house, but occasionally he would go off and return drunk. During his periods of drunkenness he would go into Ignacia and Antonio's bedroom at night and scream profanities at them. It was very frightening for the Urias children. Ignacia would send one of her sons to get Francisco Terrazas, who was able to calm Miguel. Because Francisco lived only a block away, he was able to get there quickly.

Miguel had these bad episodes roughly every three months and, at their worst, they would last a day or two. On good days he went out on the back porch and read the newspaper. On his best days he sometimes read his papers in the backyard. Miguel was an intelligent man and he often helped his nephews with their algebra and geometry homework.

My mother told us that Tío Miguel was often locked in his room. However, Maria Muñoz emphatically denied this. She said that Miguel was always free to leave the house and return at his will. It was difficult for her to understand how this could have happened to her uncle. She felt remorse that he never sat down to eat with the family, that such an intelligent man had become so isolated. He never participated in any family functions. He was ostracized by his family. The only time his siblings spoke to him was when he was drunk and had upset the family. As Maria Muñoz recalled, his was a life wasted.

Miguel Terrazas lived with the Urias family until he died on January 28, 1929. Ignacia Urias had gone to Mass early that morning. When she returned, she took him his breakfast and found that he died in his sleep. He would have been fifty-eight at the time. I found it interesting that none of his nieces could recollect his funeral.

Lupe Terrazas was known as Tía Lupita to her nieces and nephews. Tía Lupita *era sufrida*, which, according to Maria Muñoz, meant she was obligated. The actual translation means that she suffered, but Maria felt that it meant that she was obligated or perhaps obligated to suffer due to the fact that her sister had provided a home for her. She was dependent on the Urias family for food and shelter. Ignacia and Antonio didn't expect any compensation. *Sufrida,* according to Maria Muñoz, also meant serviceable and Lupita was indeed that. She helped Ignacia cook. She washed, peeled, and chopped vegetables for soup. She washed dishes at noontime during the school year. She made sure there was a fire in the stove. (Most people used wood stoves until gas lines were installed throughout the city.)

Tía Lupita was a saintly and religious woman. When Ignacia couldn't take her children to church, especially on religious holidays, Lupita would take them. During the 1920s, the Christmas *posadas* (traditional Christmas processions) were held in churches and Tía Lupita felt the Urias children should attend. She also took the children to church to give flowers to the Virgin in May. They were members of the Santa Cruz parish.

Lupita had high standards for herself and for her family. She was extremely thrifty and saved money, which she loaned or gave to relatives who were needy. This was done only after she had saved money for her own funeral. Like Miguel, she received rental income from the properties on Convent and on South Third Avenue. She inherited the properties from her father. *Era piadosa*, she was pious. She would not allow the children to criticize others. Unless they had something good to say about people, they were to keep their mouths shut. She always defended the absent party. Lupita was responsible for Miguel. She collected rent for him, bought him special foods that he liked, and took him his meals.

Tía Lupita suffered from severe *jaquecas* (migraine headaches). When one came on, she went out to a barn-like building in the Urias' backyard. This was a large building with three rooms. One of the rooms was used for chickens, another for wood, and in the third Tía Lupita would smoke *chuchupate*. This was an herb, which she crumbled and rolled up in cigarette papers. She said the chuchupate helped the headaches. This herb had a horrible smell and the Urias children avoided the shed when she suffered from the headaches. Lupita also suffered from pleurisy and always protected herself from drafts.

Not only did she help the Urias family, but also she helped her other siblings. In 1928 she went to Los Angeles to help her sister Angelita. She stayed there to help care for her brother-in-law, who was dying of cancer. She returned to Tucson for Miguel's funeral, but immediately went back to Los Angeles where her services were needed. She stayed there until her brother-in law died and the household was settled.

Lupita Terrazas returned to Tucson and to the Urias family. She continued to live with them until the time of her death. Maria Muñoz remembered that Lupita died in the bathroom. At that time she was a large woman and they had a difficult time getting her body out of the bathroom. She had saved money for her funeral so that her death would not be a burden for the family.

---

1 Sheridan, *Los Tucsonenses*, 186.

2 Ball, Phyllis. *A Photographic History of the University of Arizona, 1885–1985* (Reprint with corrections, Tucson: University of Arizona Foundation, 1987) 110.

3 *Arizona Daily Star*, 9 March 1988.

CHAPTER 5

Everyday Life

Panza llena, corazón contento.

LIFE IN TUCSON during the early part of the 1900s was not easy. Tucson may have been a city that had modern conveniences of the time, but the conveniences were primitive by today's standards. The Terrazas and Urias families lived in a close-knit Mexican-American enclave of Tucson. That group had many social mores. While the values of the Anglo population did influence the Mexican-American residents of Tucson, the Mexican-American families continued to live within their own cultural and social boundaries.

As was common throughout American culture, Mexican-American men in Tucson were responsible for the economic welfare of their families. I can't count the number of times in my life I've heard about lazy Mexicans. It is a completely untrue, culturally biased statement. During the first two decades of the twentieth century roughly 70 to 75 percent of the Mexican-American labor force in Tucson held blue-collar jobs. The remainder held white-collar positions.[1]

Both Francisco Terrazas and Antonio Urias held white-collar occupations during those years. Francisco and a partner had a neighborhood grocery store while Antonio was a salesman. Both of them had well-respected professions within their community.

As was the custom during that era, their wives primarily worked in their homes. This was no easy task; families were much larger then. Women were expected raise the children, cook, clean, do laundry, and entertain. Unmarried or widowed women were often enlisted by their extended families to help with these tasks. If families could afford it, hired help was often found. And, as children became older, they were expected to assume responsibility for specific chores around their homes.

Many of my family stories revolve around the everyday tasks done in the Urias and Terrazas households. I was indeed fortunate to have a rich oral history of what was necessary to keep a large household running. In the case of the Urias home, Ignacia was primarily responsible for keeping her home running smoothly. Her sister Lupita Terrazas was there to help her. Within the Terrazas home, Angelita Martinez was the person who managed the majority of the household chores. Virginia Terrazas divided her time between the home and helping at her husband's store.

The two biggest tasks required of women at that time, aside from caring for their children, were cooking and laundry. One can only imagine the huge amounts of food that a large family could consume during its three daily meals. People then did not have extensive wardrobes; clothing was worn for several days at a time. Laundry was done only once a week. Because of the heat, the laundry was always done outside. Most of the Mexican-American families had a cooking pit behind the home where larger items of food were cooked. However, once a week the area was reserved for doing the family laundry. Most families used one-hundred-pound-sized cans, which formerly held lard, as laundry tubs. These cans were set atop the cooking pit. Water was heated for washing and the laundry, especially towels, sheets, and white clothes, was boiled and bleached.[2] The other clothing was done after the white clothes had been cleaned and the water cooled. A washboard was used for scrubbing the clothes. Laundry was hung on clotheslines in backyards to dry. This was a daylong task. Both the Terrazas and Urias families had young women who would come in and help with the laundry. It was a wonderful day indeed when the families were finally able to purchase the newly invented wringer washing machines. At that point, the children were expected to help do laundry.

Food and its preparation were extremely important for the Mexican-American families of Tucson. The cooking of specific foods revolved around certain times of the year. These included holidays, birthdays or Saint's days, and the growing season of certain fruits and vegetables.

The ethnic food prepared and eaten by the Mexican-American residents of Tucson was and continues to be that of the Sonoran region.

The primary ingredients used are red and green chiles. The other important staples are flour and corn tortillas, pinto beans that form the base for *frijoles,* and rice. It is a shame that in our family many of these recipes were not written down and saved. We were always taught to make these dishes by visualization, adding a little of this, and a little of

Standing, left to right: Gonzalo, Lupe, Brígida, Ignacia, Antonio.
Seated, left to right: Maria, Antonio (Tony), Gilberto, Armida, Celia, Ignacio.   *1918*
<small>Photo courtesy of Celia Diaz</small>

that. We were taught to know if things looked right, were the correct consistency, had the right flavor.

Huge pots of beans were always kept cooking by every Mexican family. They were the mainstay of the diet and could be eaten at most any meal. Children were expected to help sort and clean the beans. There were always small pebbles that had to be removed as well as those beans that were shriveled or broken. Once this was done, the beans were rinsed and then soaked overnight. The next day the beans were simmered with either a piece of salt pork or a ham hock, salt, pepper, onion, and garlic. Occasionally, baking soda was added (to decrease flatulence). It took hours for the beans to cook and their wonderful aroma filled the homes.

Pinto beans were prepared in several ways. The easiest manner was to serve them in their broth, to which vinegar, onions, garlic, and *chile tepines* (small red peppers) were added. We called these *frijoles vaqueros*. But the most traditional way to serve the frijoles was to refry them. The broth was strained off and reserved. The beans were mashed. Lard was heated in a skillet and the mashed beans were added. In my family, not only was the reserved broth used with the beans, but milk was also added to the mashed beans. When the mixture reached the desired smooth consistency, cheese was added as the final touch. Frijoles were served with the rest of a meal, or used as a main dish with *tortillas de harina* (flour tortillas).

I must mention here that lard was a primary ingredient used in Mexican cooking. Because of medical advances we no longer recommend using lard. But there is something about it that enhances the flavor of frijoles, *arroz* (rice), *tamales, tacos*, and *enchiladas*. Although all of the above foods can be made without lard, there is still something about the way that it enhances the flavors of these foods that is missed when it is not used.

Arroz is another dish used with many meals. Although not as necessary as frijoles, it is nonetheless important. Our family prepares the rice by sautéing it in lard until it turns bright white. At that point hot water is added, just enough to cover the rice. While that is being brought to a boil, a tomato sauce is made. The sauce is composed of tomato juice, a small amount of diced tomato, chicken broth or water, onion, garlic, salt, and pepper. This mixture is added to the rice. As soon as the rice begins to boil, it is covered, the heat is turned to low, and it is cooked roughly fifteen to twenty minutes. This ensures that the rice will be fluffy, not gummy.

When I was a child, people always used to ask me what kind of food I ate. I thought it was rather offensive. What kind of food did I eat? The same thing everyone else ate. Just because we were Mexican-American did not mean we ate only beans and tortillas. Baked chicken, roast beef, and soups were part of our diet along with ethnic or traditional Mexican dishes. My mother told me she had been asked the same thing when she was growing up. She had given the same answer.

There are certain of our ethnic Mexican dishes that have special places in our family gatherings. Specific holidays are synonymous with specific foods. This was as true in the early part of the twentieth century as it is today. The women always prepared the food. The preparation itself was a very social event. It was not done by just one person, but often several women, *tías* from the extended family, gathered to prepare the food.

The most important and time-consuming thing to prepare was tamales. I too can remember being a part of a family gathering to make tamales. Tamales are the principle dish that is served for Christmas. Maria Muñoz and Celia Diaz were able to recall how their mother, Ignacia Terrazas Urias, carried out this process. The same method was used by my mother's family and by countless other families in Tucson during the early 1900s.

Ignacia Terrazas Urias made tamales with her sister Lupita. Virginia Terrazas helped her mother, Angelita Martinez, make tamales for their family. When their daughters were old enough to be of help, usually around age ten, they were allowed to participate and thus the skill was passed on to the next generation.

In the Urias household it took several days of preparation to make the tamales. Two *sartas* (strings) of red chile were cleaned, roasted, boiled, and ground. Roughly twenty-five pounds of beef and pork were cut into one-inch cubes. The meat was sautéed, combined with the red chile sauce, and chopped green olives were added. The next step was to process the *hojas* (cornhusks). The hojas were soaked and cleaned in hot water to make them pliable.

Then the *masa* was prepared. Before machines were made to process masa (kernels of corn) it was done by hand. This was very painstaking and involved removing kernels of corn from cobs. Once this was done the kernels were ground by food grinders into a puree. Roughly three-quarters to one pound of lard was added to four pounds of masa. The lard was first creamed until it formed peaks or made *ojitos* (floated) when it was dropped in water. This was a huge task as the lard was beaten by hand. Salt and a small amount of sugar were added. These women never measured amounts, but taste-tested the product before rolling up the tamales. The masa was added gradually to the creamed lard along with some of the stock in which the meat had been cooked. This gave the masa flavor and good consistency. The older children were then enlisted in *untando los tamales* (thinly spreading the masa on the corn husks). Once the masa had been put on the husks, the meat with red chile was spread. It was topped with a green olive and often a slice of jalapeno. The tamales were then wrapped and were ready to be steamed. The tamales had to be cooked immediately as both the masa and the chile mixture could spoil easily. Today the tamales may be frozen until they are to be served. This gives the cook ample time to prepare them. But in days gone by this painstaking task had to be done within a matter of days.

The tamales favored by the Terrazas family are green corn tamales. These tamales are always made in the summer when the green corn is available. There is a very small window of time when the corn can be obtained and processed into masa. Green corn comes from a certain place in the state of Sonora. The green corn itself must be very tender because if it is too tough the masa will be dry. The corn is ground into masa and lard is then added. These tamales are a completely different consistency than the red chile tamales; the masa is very smooth and almost creamy. When the masa is the correct consistency it can be spread on the hojas. Once the masa has been spread, diced green chile and grated jack cheese are spooned on the center. The hojas are then wrapped and ready to be steamed. The hojas for green corn tamales must be fresh and not dried. If dried, the tamales will take on the flavor of the dry husk and won't be edible. Green corn tamales are the crème de la crème of tamales for families of Sonoran heritage. As with the other tamales, making them is very time and labor intensive but completely worthwhile.

Hojas that cover the tamales have been a slight joke with the Terrazas family. As a matter of fact, I have even done this myself. When one serves tamales to guests who are eating them for the first time, one must explain how to remove the hoja. It is merely there as a container, it protects the masa and filling during the steaming process. The tamale must be unwrapped and the hoja discarded. Occasionally it can be fun to watch the uninitiated attempt to eat a tamale, hoja and all. This joke is usually reserved for good friends or for new in-laws and is, in a way, an initiation into our family.

One of my favorite memories about helping make tamales revolves around Cruzita. Cruzita was a woman who cared for my grandmother when she was elderly. Not only did Cruzita perform that task, she cooked, cleaned, and was a beloved companion and family friend. When I was an adolescent and was allowed to help make tamales, Cruzita was the primary cook. While we were working she used to say jokingly, "I have made so many tamales in my life that when I die I will be wrapped in a hoja and buried."

Menudo was another traditional food, which was made and served for New Year's. In the early days the *panza, tripas*, and *patas* (stomach, tripe, and hooves) of beef were sold without being cleaned. Cleaning was a huge chore, which was often given to boys in the family. A frame was constructed on which the panza was hung. Using a solution of lye, the boys had to scrub the panza with stiff-bristled brushes until clean. They were given several rinsings in water until clear. A hundred-pound lard can was set over a cooking fire in the backyard. The can was filled with water and the panza, tripas, and patas, which had been cut into bite-sized pieces, were added. Cloves of garlic were the next ingredients to be put into the mixture. *Nixtamal*, corn kernels treated with lye or lime to remove the outer skin, were washed and rinsed till the water came clear. These were added to the can and then the menudo simmered for hours and hours.

Menudo was always served on New Year's Eve and Day. An old wife's tale stated that it was a good cure for a hangover. Everyone loved menudo. Everyone but me, of course. I could never stand the thought of eating tripe. I could never stand to go inside my grandmother's house when menudo was being cooked. The odor of the cooking menudo was enough to make me gag. It was something I was teased about by my cousins. You weren't a true Mexican unless you liked menudo.

Posole was something I loved. It is similar to menudo, but without the tripas. Posole is made with pinto beans, which are rinsed, soaked, and then cooked. Oxtail and hominy are added to the beans. It must be cooked all day in order for the oxtail to become tender and fall off the bone. It is seasoned with onion, garlic, salt, and pepper. Once it is ready chile tepines are added. Posole has the most delicious aroma. When I was young I could never understand why people would prefer menudo to posole.

Lengua (tongue), served in either *pipian* (a tomato and red chile sauce) or as a salad, was a delicacy. The tongue was boiled until it was tender, usually about three hours. The tough outer skin was removed and the tongue was thinly sliced. Pipian was made of red chile sauce thickened with ground toasted pumpkin seeds. The thinly sliced tongue was then mixed into the pipian.

Another way to serve tongue was *salpicón* (also called *fiambre*), which was more like a salad or terrine. Steamed and sliced potatoes, carrots, beets, and green beans were dipped into a marinade of vinegar and mustard along with sliced boiled eggs. The tongue was also thinly sliced and placed in the center of a serving platter, which was lined with lettuce to make the dish more attractive. The vegetables and eggs were arranged around the tongue. It was chilled until firm, but was served at room temperature. Salpicón was a very pretty dish and one that accomplished cooks enjoyed preparing.

Enchiladas Sonorenses were a special meal. Masa was prepared into two- to three-inch rounds about three-eights of an inch thick. The enchiladas were fried in lard and then drained. While still warm they were completely dipped into *chile colorado* (red chile sauce). They were placed on a plate, sprinkled with *queso requesón* (white cheese), sliced green olives, and sliced green onions. They were always served with rice and frijoles. It was most common for each person to receive three enchiladas.

Soups were also important meals. There were all sorts of soups, but the most popular with the Terrazas family were *caldo de queso, pollo con arroz, sopa de fideo* (vermicelli), and *albondigas*. Caldo de queso was a potato soup. The soup was made by boiling cubed potatoes. When these were not quite done, a tomato sauce made with onions, garlic, salt, pepper, and diced tomatoes was added along with diced green chile. Immediately before the soup was served grated jack cheese was liberally sprinkled on top. Pollo con arroz was simply chicken with rice soup, but had a tomato base. The fideo was usually a chicken and tomato broth with small pieces of chicken, vegetables, and broken vermicelli. Albondigas is a soup with large meatballs in a beef broth with garlic, onions, and cilantro. The meatballs are prepared with ground beef, rice, and spices. The meatballs are sautéed and then added to the beef broth. It is still a great favorite. All of these sopas were served with *tortillas de harina* (flour tortillas).

Sonoran-style tortillas, flour tortillas, were made on a daily basis. There were two types of flour tortillas, *gorditas* and regular tortillas. Gorditas were tortillas that were about eight inches in diameter. They were used in place of bread at almost every meal. Regular flour tortillas were more labor intensive. These tortillas are paper thin, lacy, and roughly eighteen inches in diameter. These tortillas are always used for making burritos, which were filled with frijoles and other meat mixtures such as *birria, carne seca*, and *carne de res*. One of my mother's favorite gringo stories was about the Sonoran tortillas. The tortillas were always folded into rectangles and placed next to plates. The Terrazas family never told the gringos what the tortillas were, but loved to watch while the unsuspecting guest would carefully unfold the tortilla and place it in their lap, thinking it was a napkin. The family members would then burst into laughter and explain to the poor, humiliated guest how the tortilla was to be used.

Carne (beef) was prepared by methods that made it easy to keep and to prevent spoilage. Meat had to be prepared by these methods because our great-grandmothers had no refrigeration. *Carne seca* (dried beef) was made from thin strips of meat that were salted, hung, and dried in a special screened box. The box was covered with cheesecloth to protect the beef from flies. The strips of beef had to be turned regularly to become cured. When finished it was almost like a beef jerky and kept until it was needed. *Carne machaca* (dried, shredded beef) was prepared by pounding beef on a *metate* (a stone slab similar to a mortar and pestle). Once the beef had been pounded into small pieces tomato and red chile sauce were added and it became known as carne machaca. *Carne asada* was also used. For this dish, beef was broiled and then shredded before being served with tortillas. The family also liked *chorizo*, a sausage made of beef and/or pork, which was sautéed with eggs and served in tortillas.

When my mother, Amalia Terrazas, was young she was very thin and her grandmother was afraid she was anemic. She made a dish that made my mother cringe. She said that her grandmother would buy cattle blood from butcher. She would cook it in a cast-iron skillet with onions, garlic, salt, and pepper. She sautéed it, stirring constantly, until it thickened or curdled. She would then force the children to eat it. My mother likened it to eating liver and said that it made her gag.

In the early twentieth century chickens were scarcely seen at meat markets in Tucson. People usually kept their own chickens so they would have fresh eggs. Chickens were killed when they were getting old or when they were a nuisance. Almost every family that their own chicken coop and slaughtered chickens as needed. In the 1930s, as refrigeration became less of an issue, it was more common to find chickens and eggs in markets. A chicken coop in the backyard was no longer a necessity and a further sign of social progress.

Special beverages have their place on our family history, as well. *Champurro* or *champurrado* was a thick, hot chocolate drink often made on cold winter nights. Sometimes it was thickened with corn masa, sometimes with flour or cornstarch. It was usually made with milk, but if that was scarce it could be made with water. It was sweetened with sugar and flavored with cinnamon and was a favorite drink among children. *Atole* was a rice-based drink and was prepared similarly to champurro. It too was served primarily during the winter. *Teswin* was the drink favored by adults. This was an alcoholic beverage that was made by mixing fresh pineapple juice with *panocha* (blocks of brown cane sugar) and allowing it to ferment. It had a little kick and one had to develop a taste for this drink. Teswin was usually served during family gatherings, birthdays, and holidays.

Common desserts were pies, baked apples, and rice pudding, which were sometimes served with applesauce or crushed pineapple. Fresh fruit was often not available in Tucson so dried fruit such as apples, peaches, and apricots were used. *Empanadas*, which are turnovers, were made of panocha or pumpkin. *Empanadas de calabaza* (pumpkin turnovers) were a favorite with the Urias family. *Sopapilla*s were popular with both the Urias and Terrazas children. They were served with cinnamon and sugar or with honey. *Bizcochuelos* were cookies that were so light they would almost melt in one's mouth. They were flavored with anise seed and were usually made for special days such as birthdays or holidays. Angel food cakes were baked on Saturday for Sunday dessert.

Mealtimes were special times that families took to sit down and go over the day's events. They were very important as far as the family being together. Food was made to enjoy, but it had to be practical as well. Many foods were seasonal and were served for special celebrations. Certain foods and their preparation became social events. They continue to have the same meaning for the Terrazas family today. Certain people have made efforts to continue family traditions associated with foods. Tamales, frijoles, albondigas, and many of the carne dishes are made now, not with recipes, but from scratch with memories handed down from our mothers. Other things, such as tortillas, can be easily purchased. However, certain dishes are lost, as has been the case with lengua. It is not something one commonly sees, or even thinks to prepare.

As with everything else, things evolve and change with the times. Some foods will always remain part of family tradition, although the preparation may change due to convenience. Some dishes will be lost because people no longer have a liking for them. And still other foods will evolve because it is what is in vogue for that period of time. But what won't change is the importance that is attached to specific foods and how they relate to certain groups or cultures.

BISCOCHUELOS
Courtesy of Celia Diaz and Maria Muñoz

½ cup *manteca de rez*
   (rendered beef suet)
1½ cups sugar
½ cup water
6 cups flour
½ teaspoon salt

4 teaspoons cinnamon
2 tablespoons cornstarch
1 teaspoon ground anise seed
1 pound lard
8 egg yolks

To make the manteca de rez, place a piece of beef suet in a skillet and heat until the fat liquifies. Pour off the fat and let it solidify before using.

Pour the sugar into a bowl and cover with the water. Let stand for at least 1 hour. Sift together 2 cups of the flour and the salt, cinnamon, cornstarch, and anise.

Cream the lard and manteca de rez until soft peaks form. Add the sugar mixture and cream well. Add the egg yolks one at a time and mix well. Gradually add the flour mixture, mixing until blended. Add the remaining flour 1 cup at a time mixing until well blended. If the mixture is too soft 1 more cup of flour may be added.

Form the dough into small balls. Roll each ball on a hard surface until it reaches a cigarette shape and is roughly 3½ inches long. Shape into an O and pinch the ends together. Bake on ungreased cookie sheets at 425° for 10 to 15 minutes or until golden brown. Makes 10–12 dozen cookies.

I decided to try this recipe and made a few changes. This recipe did not call for ground anise, but my mother always used it in her biscochuelos. I don't like anise, so I added only a small amount. When the cookies came out of the oven, I let them cool for 5 minutes, then rolled them in cinnamon and sugar. I never liked biscochuelos when I was a child. They were very hard and I didn't like the anise seed. Maria Muñoz told me that her mother made wonderful biscochuelos that would melt in your mouth. When she was in high school she helped her mother make these cookies and carefully wrote down the amounts of ingredients. These cookies are nothing like those made by my mother. They do melt in your mouth! I don't like the amount of animal fat they contain, but the flavor is wonderful. I've decided to make them for my family for Christmas.

✳

Empanadas
Courtesy of Delia Molina

1 16-ounce can Libby's pumpkin	3 tablespoons sugar
1 teaspoon cinnamon	½ teaspoon salt
¾ cup sugar	½ cup shortening
3 cups flour	½ cup milk
2 teaspoons baking powder	

Mix together the pumpkin, cinnamon, and sugar and set aside. Mix and sift the dry ingredients. Cut in the shortening, adding enough milk to hold the dough together.

On a floured surface roll out the dough to a ⅛-inch thickness, then cut into rounds 3 to 4 inches in diameter. Spoon 1 tablespoon of the pumpkin mixture onto a round of dough, placing it off to one edge. Moisten the edges with cold water then fold the round in half, pressing the edges together to seal. Bake at 375° for 15 to 20 minutes or until golden brown. Makes about 16 turnovers.

Red Chile Tamales
Courtesy of Delia Molina

5 pounds pork butt roast

2 pounds long red chile

1 teaspoon garlic powder

1 tablespoon salt

5 pounds prepared, not dry, masa
(available in Hispanic markets)

2 pounds lard

1 package clean hojas

¾ cup green whole green olives

¾ to 1 cup sliced jalapeno peppers

Cut the pork into 1-inch cubes and simmer 1 hour in 4 quarts of water. Let cool, then drain and reserve the liquid. Shred the pork and chill.

Clean the chiles and remove the tops and seeds. Simmer in 3 quarts of water for 1 hour. Put the mixture into a blender and mix until smooth.

Mix together 1 cup of the pork broth and 1½ cups of the blended chiles and set aside. Mix together the shredded pork and remaining chile, stirring until the pork is evenly coated with the chile. Add the garlic powder and 2 teaspoons of the salt.

Add the lard, remaining teaspoon of salt, and 3½ cups of the reserved pork broth to the masa. Beat with an electric mixer until a small piece of the masa mixture floats to the top when dropped into a glass of water.

Spread a thin layer of the masa mixture on the lower half of an hoja, holding it back from the bottom inch of the hoja. Spoon 1–2 tablespoons of the pork mixture onto the center of masa and top with 1 green olive and a slice of jalapeno chile. Fold one side of the hoja over the other, then fold the narrow end up.

Place the assembled tamales on a rack. Fill the bottom of a large kettle with water, no higher than the rack. Place the rack with the tamales in the kettle, cover, and steam for ½ hour. Makes 5½ dozen tamales.

*

ARROZ
Beth McCauslin

1 tablespoon olive oil
1 cup long-grain rice
¼ cup finely chopped onion

1 teaspoon finely chopped garlic
2 cups chicken broth
1 can (14½ ounces) diced tomatoes,
    reserve liquid

Heat the oil in a heavy sauce pan. Add the rice and sauté until the rice blanches. Add the onion and garlic and cook until soft. Add the chicken broth and the reserved tomato juice to the pan along with 2 tablespoons of the diced tomatoes. Add salt and pepper to taste. Bring the mixture to a boil and cover. Turn heat to low and simmer for 20 minutes.

ENCHILADAS SONORENSES
Beth McCauslin

FOR THE ENCHILADAS:

2 pounds prepared (not dry) masa
   (available in Hispanic markets)
1 egg
1 teaspoon salt
½ teaspoon baking powder
1½ cups grated Monterrey Jack
   cheese
2 cans (10 ounces each) red
   enchilada sauce

FOR THE GARNISH:

Shredded lettuce
Queso requeson (Mexican white cheese)
Sliced green onions
Sliced green olives

Mix all the enchilada ingredients together and set aside for 1 hour, but do not refrigerate. Divide the masa into 12 equal-sized balls. Flatten each ball and pat into a 3½-inch round.

Meanwhile, heat the lard in a deep skillet until smoking, the lard should be ¼ to ½ inch deep. Cook the enchiladas on each side until golden colored, turning once (about 2 to 3 minutes on each side). Remove from the skillet and drain on several layers of paper towels. Keep the enchiladas warm.

Heat the red enchilada sauce in a pan. When hot, dip each enchilada into the sauce until entirely covered, then place it on a platter. Spoon additional sauce over the tops of the enchiladas. Place a thin layer of sliced lettuce over the enchiladas. Sprinkle liberally with queso requeson, sliced green onions, and sliced green olives.

CHAPTER 6

Family Gatherings

Mi casa es su casa.

IN THE EARLY TWENTIETH CENTURY extended family and friends were the social fabric that held the Mexican-American population of Tucson together. Not only did they serve to keep the family together, but they also perpetuated the culture and allowed it to flourish within the Anglo-controlled city.

The Catholic religion is the foundation for the family within the Mexican culture. The laws of the Catholic Church govern all of life's activities. Almost all social events revolved around church functions. Christmas, Easter, and saint's feast days were not only special days for the church, but for the family as well.

Births, baptisms, marriages, and deaths were intimately interwoven with the Catholic Church and the Mexican families. Everyone attended mass on Sundays and holy days. Many people, especially women, attended mass on a daily basis. Sundays were the day that was owed to the Lord. That was not a day for work, but one that was saved for God.

On Sunday, the most important event of the day was to attend mass. The whole family went, although sometimes the women would go first thing in the morning so that they could get started on their preparations for the day. The Urias family attended Santa Cruz Church on 22nd Street. The Terrazas family attended St. Augustine's Cathedral. However, once All Saints Church was opened both families became members of that parish.

It mattered not which family was hosting the Sunday gathering. The house still had to be spotless and food had to be prepared. The women and children of each household were expected to perform these tasks.

The social events did not take place each Sunday, but the families went through similar routines. The house was cleaned on Saturday, the family attended mass on Sunday morning, and the women prepared the midday meal.

If it was the family's turn to host the Sunday gathering, the family would have a light meal at noon, but the main meal would be reserved for guests in the late afternoon or early evening. The adults mingled and gossiped; children were expected to play outside. The women were usually in one room and the men in another. If children invaded their domain, they were usually allowed to stay for a short while, but were then escorted outside to rejoin their playmates.

Our families continue to have gatherings and, although people and circumstances change with the times, there are some things that remain unaltered. Even as a child I remember these gatherings as being fairly loud. There was always laughter and occasionally heated debates – usually about politics. And someone was always checking on the children. It was a very festive, noisy atmosphere. There usually seemed to be a supply of beer, which only made the voices more animated.

Dinner was always one of the highlights of the event. Afterward, the women would retire to the kitchen and do the cleaning. All of the women helped with this task. When this was done the real fun would start. In my grandparents' time, before the advent of television, games were played, stories were told, and there was music.

The men loved to play cards and their favorite game was called *malilla*, which is similar to pinochle. At the Urias gatherings malilla was usually played while the women were cleaning the kitchen. There was only one woman who played the game with the men and her name was Doña Carmen Valenzuela. She was a widow and very outspoken. She was witty and made lots of jokes so there was much laughter during these games.

The Terrazas family enjoyed playing cards also. Bertha Terrazas Rodriquez recalled a time when her father, Francisco, wanted to play cards. He was so adamant about it that he went to the Lyric Theater, ran down the aisle until he found the couple with whom he wanted to play cards, and escorted them to his home. My mother, Amalia Terrazas Goodman, told my siblings and me that she had heard that her father was quite a cardplayer. In fact, she told us that she had heard that he was a big gambler in Tucson until after World War II.

Then, as now, children were expected to play outside. They were not to interfere with the adult groups who were usually discussing family matters, which they considered inappropriate for children. The only exception was the very young, who needed to be with their mothers. Their older siblings watched even toddlers. In the past when the children weren't outside playing they were usually in a bedroom telling ghost stories. Now they are outside playing games or inside watching television or videos.

The gatherings always ended with music. At the Urias home their eldest daughter, Brígida, played the piano and Antonio Urias played the flute. At the Terrazas' several of the children played the piano and Francisco played the guitar or mandolin. Francisco and Virginia Terrazas had beautiful voices. They would sing duets, which included "La Golondrina," "La Paloma," and "Los Ojos Negros." They also danced and were said to be a lovely couple on the dance floor.

After the music, it was time to go home. Guests never left without helping put things away. Helping was one of the things that children were taught and it was something that was expected. To be invited into a home and not offer to help with the preparation, serving, or cleaning afterwards was considered to be extremely rude. Thanking the hosting family was always the last thing that was done before leaving. This also was a requisite and was necessary in order to be invited to return.

Women also had their own gatherings. These were often held on weekdays in the morning and coffee was always served. These were fairly informal and often meant just dropping by to check and see how the family was doing. These were always very supportive visits with much advice being offered. Husbands and children were the primary topics. I always found them to be settings that offered a great deal of teaching, especially regarding childcare or parenting.

All of these events were family gatherings. Everyone attended, from the smallest infant to the very elderly – all were expected to participate. Great attention was paid to those two groups. The very old held special positions and were treated with ultimate respect. In the Mexican culture the elderly are revered as we can learn from their experience. They are treated with politeness and utmost respect as they have given us our heritage. At gatherings they usually held the seat of honor, which meant

Francisco, Maria Luisa, and Virginia Terrazas. *1912*
PHOTO COURTESY OF ARIZONA HISTORICAL SOCIETY, TUCSON
Courtesy of the Arizona Historical Society/Tucson. 91657

they were served their meals first and they sat in the best seats. Infants and young children were pampered and coddled even while we recognized that the children were there to learn from the adults. It is the children who will be there to carry on our family traditions after we are gone. Thus, all age groups are incorporated into and become integral members of these social gatherings.

Although our family gatherings have changed, there are still elements that remain the same, even today. The family now gathers for events such as holidays, birthdays, graduations, and reunions for returning relatives. Women still gather to discuss their families and share experiences. There is still coffee, the meal, and talking. It is a supportive experience to be shared by family and close friends.

What we are missing today is the oral history – people today don't tell the stories. Our forbearers didn't have television, but they did have wonderful songs, stories, and games, which they passed on to their children. There are so many of them and they are rich in culture, tradition, and history. Now it is our turn to pass these stories on to our children and continue this tradition.

CHAPTER 7

The Iceman and Other Pranks

Dime con quién anda y te dire quién eres.

WHAT DID CHILDREN in Tucson do in the early part of the 1900s to amuse themselves? How did they keep themselves occupied when not in school, especially during the long, hot, and dusty summers? That seemed to be no problem for them because, as children have always done, they invented things. They used their ingenuity and came up with things to keep themselves busy.

What the Terrazas children came up with was usually a game – games that always had a measure of suspense and fear of discovery. The basic goal was to avoid punishment at all costs, especially discovery and punishment by their mother. To accomplish this goal was a major feat of bravery and demanded the respect of the children.

The Terrazas children had their leader in Delia. She was extremely outgoing and curious. It was she who came up with adventures for not only her siblings, but often her cousins as well. The children would follow her lead – sometimes by coercion – but they knew she would always come up with something exciting.

In 1879 ice, which was a luxury and a necessity, arrived in Tucson. Between 1875 and 1876, Paul Maroney began sending for the equipment needed to build Tucson's first ice plant in Levine's Park.[1] Machinery was brought from Colton, California, to Tucson by ferry over the Colorado River and then by freight wagon drawn by sixteen mules. Once the building and the machinery had been installed, ice was produced and distribution began in 1879.

The process of making ice was interesting. Water was taken from a well by a steam pump. A machine was then used to lower the temperature of a non-congealable liquid such as common ether, mephitic ether, or sulfurous oxide. These liquids were run through a rotating coil in a cylinder, then into a freezing tank in which containers of water that were to be converted into ice were placed. The temperature of the non-congealable liquid was lower and a condenser at the opposite end of the tank carried off the vaporous gases. The water that was circulated became frozen. It took 48 hours to produce 3,500 pounds of ice.

The ice was stored in icehouses, which were specially built to resist high temperatures in summer months. The ceilings were six feet from the roof. The space between the roof and the ceiling was packed with hay as were all the spaces that surrounded the rooms. Before the ice was to be delivered it was cut into blocks.[2]

By the 1920s ice for Tucson was supplied by the Arizona Ice and Cold Storage, which was located at 65 Toole Avenue. Employees would be up at 4:45 A.M. to go to the ice docks. The men would load blocks weighing twenty-five to one hundred pounds into the trucks. By 5:15 A.M. they were loaded and on their routes. When they were within a block of their routes, they'd blow the truck whistles. The whistle was connected to the exhaust pipe and sounded like a train whistle. Customers needed the ice delivered in the early mornings before it melted. Most home iceboxes took twenty-five-pound blocks. Ice was delivered twice a day, seven days a week.[3]

Children loved the slivers of ice that could be found in the truck beds. Delia Terrazas made quite a game of this. The trucks moved slowly down the streets making door-to-door deliveries. She challenged her siblings to jump onto the truck, grab as many slices of ice as they could, then jump off the truck without being caught. This could be done while the driver was making a delivery or while the truck was actually in motion. Since the trucks moved quite slowly it was possible to jump onto the truck bed, grab the ice, and then jump down again without being caught. If her siblings refused to participate in this game, Delia would coerce them by threatening to kick their shins or pull their hair. She was quite a force to deal with. Her siblings feared her, but respected and admired her for standing up to their overbearing mother.

Delia Terrazas was always more impressed if the children could get ice while the truck was in motion. Of course just getting ice was a challenge, but not getting caught was the biggest thrill. If caught and reported to their mother by the iceman, they would receive a tongue-lashing and a spanking. It was the thrill of risk taking that the Terrazas children loved, so they always took up Delia's challenge. According to my mother they were rarely caught.

The other prank the Terrazas children liked to do was to spy on the prostitutes living on Sabino Alley. Before 1918 Sabino Alley was also known as Gay Alley and was located between Ochoa and McCormick Streets to the north and south and was bordered by Meyers and Convent on the west and east.[4] This was known to be a rough district and no respectable woman had any business venturing within its boundaries. This area was actually within a very short walk of the Terrazas Grocery Store. The fact that it was off limits to children made it all the more tempting.

Terrazas Grocery. Francisco Terrazas in center.   *1923*

It was the practice at the turn of the century for young single women to live in boarding houses if they didn't live with their relatives. Occasionally these boarding houses or individual homes were actually brothels and the Gay/Sabino Alley area had been noted to be the sporting or red light district of Tucson at that time.[5] Amalia Goodman said that it was known in the 1920s as the red light district because the establishments that offered prostitution always displayed red lights in their front windows.

According to Fresia Terrazas Lindberg the Terrazas children went to the family grocery store every morning. There they had breakfast with their parents. Before going to school they had to help get orders ready for delivery. When they had to help make deliveries, they would fight over who made deliveries to which homes. There were two places in particular in which they were interested – the home of Mrs. Tempy Harris and the boarding home owned by *La Jirafa* (The Giraffe).

I have never been able to discover the true identity of La Jirafa or her address, but I was told that she lived in Sabino Alley. My mother told me that La Jirafa ran a brothel and had women working for her. She was described as a black woman who was called La Jirafa because she had a very long neck. My mother said she was one of the most homely women she had ever met, but that she had beautiful hands and was very kind. She also had a diamond embedded in one of her teeth. She told the children that if she ever needed money, she had it on her person and that no one could ever steal it from her. La Jirafa was married to a mulatto who was half Indian and half black.[6] According to Amalia Terrazas Goodman, La Jirafa was from the South and college educated. Because of prejudice at that time she was unable to find a job as a teacher and had to turn to prostitution to support herself. She was bright, had good business sense, and developed a profitable business.

Tempy Harris lived with her husband, William, at 62 Cushing Street directly across from the Terrazas Grocery. William was a porter on the Southern Pacific Railroad.[7] According to Bertha Terrazas Rodriquez, Tempy was a "colored woman" who was married, but had a *mestizo* (half Mexican, half Anglo) lover. She always entertained the man when her husband was out of town.

The Terrazas children had to deliver groceries to both La Jirafa and Tempy Harris. They would fight over the privilege of going up to the doors and personally delivering the boxes, which would enable them to look into the homes. Delia made a game of having the children peek into the windows to try to see something scandalous. If they were caught, they were severely reprimanded by the women. La Jirafa's home in Sabino Alley was not safe as there were often brawls and stabbings. If she caught the children, she would lecture them about being in an unsafe place and walk them back to their father's store. If Francisco Terrazas was there, he would merely scold the children. Heaven help them if Virginia was there. Not only had they gotten in trouble, where they had been and what they were doing was completely scandalous and unacceptable. A severe punishment was in store, hence the challenge for Delia. To peek in a window and not be caught was truly a thrill.

What exactly happened if the Terrazas children were caught and punished? Their mother was the disciplinarian. Virginia Terrazas was quick to find blame and punish. All of the Terrazas children were aware of her judgments so all of their actions were governed by how she would react. This was also true in almost all aspects of their home life. The goal was to stay out of her way, to attempt things without being caught, and to avoid punishment at all costs.

Most of the children were able to stay out of her way. But Delia seemed to be the one child that antagonized her more than the others. Her punishments were more harsh and occurred frequently. Virginia made her kneel on the floor and hold her arms out, and then placed a rock in each outstretched hand. She then had to pray the rosary. When Virginia was gone and out of earshot, Delia would put the rocks down. One of her siblings always had to stand guard to warn her if Virginia was coming and put the rocks back on her outstretched palms.

Virginia also used a green switch cut from a tree in their yard. She would hit the children on the back of their legs. But worse of all were the tongue-lashings she would give. Screaming loudly, she would inform the child why what she or he had done was improper, then demand to know why the child had committed the wrongdoing. She always finished by making the child feel guilty about what had occurred. Guilt is a very powerful form of intimidation within the Mexican culture. Children are made to feel guilty about hurting or embarrassing their parents and it is a very powerful form of control. Virginia Terrazas was a master at controlling her children through guilt.

These tongue-lashings were often so severe that Delia went to stay with the Urias family for a few days. It was not uncommon for her to go to their home to recover from her mother's spite. Zarina was another of Virginia's targets. Their Urias cousins remember the two of them having to retreat to the Urias home to be comforted by their aunt, Ignacia. While there, Ignacia, called Tía Nachita by the children, attempted to restore their self-confidence and make them feel loved. Because of this the Terrazas children were extremely fond of her. She became their defender and role model. Amalia often wished that Ignacia was her mother. The Terrazas children feared their domineering, controlling mother.

Francisco Terrazas was just the opposite of his wife. His was always a gentle scolding with an explanation of what they had done wrong and a rationale for why the children shouldn't have acted in a certain manner. He never raised his voice, he didn't spank, he merely glared in order to command their attention. This only fueled Virginia's fury as she felt she had to be the disciplinarian of the family.

The Terrazas children had very fond memories of their father. Most of his time was spent managing his small grocery store. He always insisted that the family be together at mealtimes. The family primarily spoke Spanish at home except during their evening meal. Francisco asked each member to recall his or her day in English. With that out of the way, he proceeded to read articles from the newspaper and discuss them with the children. That was their introduction to English and to current events.

Francisco also enjoyed music. He played the mandolin and guitar and loved to sing. In the evenings he would play for the children and teach them regional songs. As they grew older most of the children sang. Frank and Rene played the guitar. Fresia and Viola went on to have voice lessons and sang with their church choir. Besides singing, Francisco taught the children to dance. The girls especially liked to take to the floor with their father. He taught them the waltz, the fox trot, and the polka.

The family had a Victrola and enjoyed listening to records. Occasionally, when Francisco and Virginia were working at the store, the children would wind up the Victrola, dance to the tunes, and hope their parents wouldn't discover their antics.[8] Zarina often organized lunches for their Urias cousins. She would make tuna sandwiches for everyone and afterwards the whole gang would listen to music and dance. The gramophone was a costly item and one that wasn't to be touched by the children. Discovery only meant another of their mother's punishments.

---

[1] *Arizona Daily Star*, 22 July 1956.

[2] *Arizona Weekly Star*, 29 January 1880.

[3] *Arizona Daily Star*, 26 July 1992.

[4] Caywood, Eugene. *A History of Tucson Transportation: The Arrival of the Railroad, Beginnings of Transit in Tucson* (Tucson: Tucson-Pima County Historical Commission, 1980), 11–12.

[5] Sonnichsen, C. L. *Tucson, The Life and Times of an American City* (Norman, Okla.: University of Oklahoma Press, 1982), 123.

[6] McCauslin, Elizabeth. Terrazas Family History, 3.

[7] Tucson City Directory, 1931.

[8] Muñoz interview, 3 May 1997.

CHAPTER 8

La Escuela

No me hagas la vida pesada.

ℰDUCATION WAS VERY VALUED within the Mexican-American community of Tucson. The first permanent public school in Tucson was opened in 1872.[1] As mentioned previously, Francisco Terrazas and his siblings had attended parochial schools operated by the Catholic Church. It is unclear why, but his children attended the Tucson public schools. Perhaps it was because they felt that the public education was a right of citizenship and of taxpayers. Or perhaps it was because the family couldn't afford to educate eight children through the parochial school system. The Urias children also attended the Tucson public schools.

The public school system in Tucson had been developed by individuals who had little or no experience in dealing with the Hispanic segment of the population. As a result, the policies of the public schools were largely unsympathetic toward the education of its Mexican-American students.[2] This is a theme that presents itself repeatedly in family stories.

The situation was not much better for black or Asian children. Asian children were allowed to attend the regular public schools. This was not the case for black children. There was a segregated school, the Dunbar Elementary School, which was in operation from 1918 to 1951. It was located on Eleventh Avenue and Second Street.[3] Although the Terrazas and Urias children were aware of the school they had no contact with any of its pupils as they were not allowed to go within the vicinity of the school.

By the late 1920s, 48 percent of the children in the Tucson Public School were of Mexican descent and 47 percent were Anglos. Roughly 2 percent of students in the Tucson Public schools were classified as Negroes and 3 percent were classified as "other," which presumably included Asian and American-Indian children.[4] I did occasionally recall the Terrazas and Urias families speaking of Asian classmates, but I have never heard them speak of American-Indian students. I was told that Tucson High School was a melting pot and that students of all races were allowed to attend classes together.

The University of Arizona had become well established as the state institution of higher education by the 1920s. The University of Arizona had officially opened on October 1, 1891. It was located three miles east of downtown Tucson. The University became a dynamic presence for the citizens of Tucson and was an integral part of the economy and the culture of the city.

The Terrazas and Urias children attended the Safford and Mansfield schools. It was never clear to me how the school boundaries were established in the late 1920s and 1930s. However, the distance between the schools was very short. Initially, mothers accompanied the children to school, but once they felt that the children were safe and comfortable

Safford Junior High School.   *1996*

with the route the children were allowed to walk in groups. As they got older the children attended Tucson High School. They were expected to walk to both junior high and high school even though they were longer distances.

The recurrent theme of the elementary school experience for both the Terrazas and Urias children was one of humiliation. Mexican-American students were severely reprimanded for speaking Spanish. Amalia Terrazas Goodman frequently related that early school years were hazardous to Spanish-speaking students. They were often spanked, their fingers were hit with rulers, or, if the teacher was lenient, they were sent to stand in a corner and made to wear a dunce cap made out of paper. Even mispronunciation of words was offensive. My mother often told of having her fingers hit with a ruler because she pronounced the word children as "shildren." She then vowed not to teach her children Spanish as their primary language so that they would never have to suffer the same humiliation she and so many other Mexican-American children did.

Maria Uriaz Muñoz spoke more eloquently of prejudices experienced within the public school system in Tucson. She had experiences throughout her school years that led her to believe that Mexican-American students were often passed over both in the classroom and in the grades they were given. It was generalized that the Mexican-American students were academically unable to succeed. The Anglo teachers were often unresponsive to them or treated them in a condescending manner. This further served to humiliate the children and limited their interaction in the classroom.

Maria was an exemplary student whose goal was to attend the University of Arizona. Many of her high school teachers tried to discourage her from even applying to college. When she graduated from high school the country was in the midst of the Depression. The Urias family couldn't afford college tuition and Maria was unable to find a job. She elected to return to high school for a fifth year and perfected her secretarial skills. Because of her outstanding academics the Dean of Girls at Tucson High School, Calanthe Brazelton, took an interest in her and helped Maria enroll in the University of Arizona. Miss Brazelton and her sister also provided financial assistance to Maria, which made it possible for her to attend the university.

During her freshman year Maria Urias was one of only five Mexican-American students attending the University of Arizona. Maria persevered despite many prejudicial views harbored by the university faculty and went on to graduate in the top 3 percent of the class of 1937.[5] Maria earned a degree in elementary and secondary education. She was one of only a handful of Mexican-Americans to graduate not only that year, but that decade.

No matter how severe the treatment of Mexican-American students might have been, the children in both the Urias and Terrazas families enjoyed school. They did have several humorous anecdotes about their early school years. During the 1920s Tucson hired four school nurses.[6] Their job was devoted to preventive health and detecting any infectious diseases. They checked for any physical defects that ranged from hearing and vision problems to flat feet. They notified public health officials of any communicable diseases such as tuberculosis, measles, or chickenpox. The school nurses also provided treatment for minor conditions such as head lice, or cooties, as the children called them.

Delia Terrazas was a very curious child. She was always doing things or going places that were out of her boundaries. One day she happened to see a group of children at school having their heads washed. The children were standing in line and out of curiosity Delia joined them. The children were lined up for treatment of head lice. The school nurses cut their hair, then washed it with kerosene, rinsed it with vinegar, and wrapped their heads in white towels. Delia did not have head lice, but when she appeared at home with her head wrapped with a white towel, Virginia Terrazas was mortified. What would the neighbors think? Naturally, Delia was punished.

The message to children, at least to the Terrazas children, was that cleanliness was next to godliness. You might not be wealthy, but anyone could afford a bar of soap and bathing was done routinely. Virginia Terrazas tried to prevent her children from encountering impetigo, head lice, and ringworm. After all, as she advised her children, these were diseases that only lower-class children developed. According to my mother, it was thought by Anglo parents that the Mexican-American children carried certain illnesses. She felt the Mexican-American children were observed more closely by school officials for any signs of infectious diseases as a result.

Education was valued in both the Terrazas and Urias families. All of the children were expected to finish high school. It was understood that a high school diploma would enable the young adults to find appropriate jobs. As a result only one person in the Terrazas family did not graduate from high school. Most of the members of the Urias family were high school graduates.

Tucson High School was the only high school in Tucson during the early part of the 1900s. It was an unsegregated school and was attended by adolescents from all cultural backgrounds and all socioeconomic levels. It offered the standard classes found at high schools across the country. During the 1920s and 1930s most students walked to the school. Besides classes, the school also provided social diversions such

"Old Main," University of Arizona.   *c. 1900*
PHOTO COURTESY OF ARIZONA HISTORICAL SOCIETY, TUCSON
Courtesy of the Arizona Historical Society/Tucson. B89870a

as sports events, extracurricular activities, and dances. School was a way to advance oneself and in both the Terrazas and Urias families it was understood that having a high school diploma was important. Tucson High was fondly remembered by all family members.

Several of the children in the Urias family attended college. In the Terrazas family only the boys were encouraged to go to college. Both Amalia and Fresia wanted to attend the University of Arizona, but it was not something their parents would allow. A college education wasn't valued for young women in their family. This was devastating for both of these young women. They, along with their sisters, were encouraged to find jobs directly after graduating from high school. It is amazing to me that the young women in the Urias family were encouraged to attend college, but that it was prohibited in the Terrazas family. Fresia Terrazas Lindberg told me that her father was the parent who was strictly opposed to continuing education for his daughters. Both Francisco and Rene Terrazas were encouraged to attend the University of Arizona. It seemed to be a privilege that was reserved for the males in the family. As a child I was shocked to learn that education could be denied to a person by virtue of their sex.

My mother always regretted not being allowed to further her education. In retrospect I often wonder if this was more related to the financial burden that would have been associated with obtaining a college education. After all, many of the Terrazas children would have graduated from high school during the Depression. Regardless, not being allowed to attend the University of Arizona was one of the greatest disappointments of her life. She compensated for that by encouraging her children to attend college.

———

[1] Sonnichsen, *Tucson*, 85.

[2] Sheridan, *Los Tucsonenses*, 219.

[3] Arizona Historical Society, 371.D898, 1987.

[4] Sheridan, *Los Tucsonenses*, 218.

[5] Holder, *Our Pioneer Family*, 96.

[6] Tucson Public Schools. Report of the Superintendent, 1921–1931. Arizona Historical Society 371.2 T 8985.

CHAPTER 9

Holiday Celebrations

Querer es poder.

As with any family, holidays were important events for the Terrazas family and also for the city of Tucson. These holidays served to define the cultural heritage of the city. Because of the largely Catholic population, many of these holidays were religious in nature, which in turn meant that they had a uniquely Hispanic flavor.

Christmas primarily revolved around the religious event. Las posadas were celebrated for nine days before Christmas. This can best be described as a procession that reenacted the search by Mary and Joseph for an inn in which Mary could give birth to the infant Jesus. Maria Urias Muñoz recalled that when she was a young child in the early 1920s the posadas were celebrated during the rosary at evening masses.[1] Between some of the mysteries there was a procession looking for an inn where the Virgin Mary could give birth to baby Jesus. Older children were usually selected to play the parts of Mary and Joseph. Beautiful canticles were sung in Spanish; "Los Peregrinos Buscaban Posada" was the most popular. Viola Terrazas remembered that by the 1930s, when she was a child, las posadas had become a community procession. Children were chosen to play the parts of Mary and Joseph while adults joined in the procession. The group would go from home to home asking for lodging for the pilgrims. The singing of the canticles in Spanish was a tradition that was continued. When they got to the last home they would be allowed entry. There they would be served hot chocolate and cookies, usually bizcochuelos. It was quite an honor to be selected as the final home and host to the procession. This tradition has been continued in the barrio district of Tucson. Viola was involved in this

Mexican tradition during the Christmas season for many years.

Christmas Eve was spent celebrating the birth of Christ. When the children were older and could obey the laws of abstinence they were allowed to attend midnight mass. It was a sort of coming-of-age when a child was allowed to attend that ceremony. The favorite part of the mass was singing Christmas carols. After mass each family went home and ate a traditional meal of tamales, accompanied by coffee or milk. Maria Muñoz recalled that all they ate were tamales – no beans, no rice.[2]

Christmas day each family usually celebrated by itself. Initially the families did not have Christmas trees; those came later. The younger Urias children were allowed to hang one of their clean white stockings on the fireplace mantel, or in the case of the Terrazas children, by the heating stove. Santa filled the stockings with an orange, an apple, nuts, and hard candy. The girls would be given dolls with wax faces and cloth bodies. The boys were given balls and marbles. When they were older the children were given roller skates. The roller skates were very popular and as the wheels wore out they were replaced by new wheels the following Christmas. They also got new socks and underwear. Sometimes they each got a new outfit. Gifts were not the main emphasis of their Christmas celebration. The thing that the children looked most forward to was their Christmas stockings.

As time went by and Christmas trees became more popular, the Mexican-American families of Tucson adopted the practice of putting a tree up in their homes. My mother recalled that the trees were rather spindly affairs and dried out quickly in the Tucson climate. However, they got into the spirit and strung popcorn and fresh cranberries to decorate the tree. They also put small candles on the branches, but kept a bucket of sand close by in case the tree started on fire. The candles were only lit on Christmas Eve and for a very short time to prevent the dry trees from catching on fire.

The Mexican-American people of Tucson also celebrated the new year. Menudo was the key element of the beginning of the celebration and was prepared several days ahead of time. It was a great day for the children when they were old enough to stay up and wait for the new year to arrive. Celia Diaz remembered that at the stroke of midnight gunshots could be heard as men fired their guns. Church bells and the bells of the fire stations were also rung. After midnight the menudo was served. The children were often encouraged to put eggs in vinegar and leave them until morning. When they woke they would check the shape of the eggs to determine their fate for the coming year. If the egg was somewhat rectangular, it might indicate a coffin or death. If the egg was slightly rectangular, it might represent the shape of a ship or travel, and so on. My mother allowed us to do this when we were children and I have to admit that I never thought the eggs changed their shape, but she only smiled and insisted that they had. On New Year's Day extended families and friends would gather. The men would play malilla, the women would chat, and the children would play games and tell stories.

Although Easter was an important religious holiday, it wasn't celebrated in the same way it is celebrated today. When I was a child I dreaded Good Friday. We were always taken to church where we had to pray the stations of the cross. My mother told us that that was what was expected and no questions were asked. She said that when she was a child they had to visit each Catholic church in town and pray the stations. She also told us that for as long as she could remember that day was known to be cloudy and windy in Tucson. She said that the sky was mourning the death of Jesus. On Easter Sunday, however, the day was always beautiful. Typically on Holy Thursday the scene of the washing of Jesus' feet by the twelve apostles was presented at the church service. On Holy Friday a sermon on *Las últimas palabras* (Jesus' last words on the cross) was given. It was also expected that families would attend mass on Saturday, *Día de Gloria* (Day of Glory). Easter Sunday was the celebration of Jesus' resurrection from the grave. Tucson did have an Easter egg hunt, which was started in 1930. It was held in the Military Plaza (now known as Armory Park) and the children of Tucson were invited to search for candy and hard-boiled eggs.[3] My mother told us that she had attended some of these Easter egg hunts, but I don't recall hearing that her family conducted these hunts themselves. However, Maria Muñoz did recall that her elder siblings would prepare baskets and hide marshmallow eggs in their yard.

One of the most memorable holidays in Tucson was *El Día de San Juan*. This celebration went back to the old presidio days. El Día de San Juan was celebrated on June 24. According to tradition, the rains of summer always began on this day. The Mexican people of Tucson felt that by praying to San Juan the rains would begin and their crops would grow. Initially, the people of Tucson would attend mass in the cathedral; they then walked to the Santa Cruz River and cleansed themselves for the festivities of the day. The primary events were a blessing of animals, cockfighting, horse racing, and *saco de gallo*. This last event involved horsemen who galloped at full speed and attempted to grab roosters that had been buried up to their heads in the sand.[4]

By the 1920s this holiday had changed significantly. It continued to be a special day and families would go to mass in the morning. My mother related that there was a special blessing of animals at this mass. After mass families would go to the Santa Cruz River where the children would play and swim in the water. Sometimes they would go to the *acequias* (irrigation ditches). At that time there were large cottonwoods on the banks of the Santa Cruz and also along the acequias. The Urias and Terrazas families would take picnic lunches and serve them in the shade of the cottonwoods. The whole family would attend, from the very young to the very old.

This tradition continued when I was a child. The Urias and Terrazas cousins would organize picnics in Sabino Canyon or Patagonia. The guest of honor was Ignacia Urias who always had a seat in the shade and presided over the picnic. Her function was to tell the family stories that would be handed down to the younger generations. When I was an adolescent I remember hearing about the arrival of the summer monsoons. But my mother always shook her head and said, "They don't understand that this is the work of San Juan." And then we were told the stories of the community celebrations that had taken place in her childhood and in the childhood of her father when Tucson was a small village.

The Fourth of July has traditionally been celebrated throughout America with parades and fireworks. The Fourth of July in Tucson was no different. Fathers and brothers were usually in charge of purchasing small firecrackers and sparklers, which were enjoyed at home. At the foot of A Mountain there was a small round swimming pool called Clearwater Pool and grounds where several types of foot races and contests were held. The merchants of Tucson would give prizes to the winners. But the best celebration in town was the fireworks held at the University of Arizona. Both the Terrazas and Urias families would take the streetcar to the university campus. Celia Diaz remembered that games would be held at the U of A football field. In the evening there was a wonderful firework display. The University of Arizona continued to play an integral role in the lives of Tucsonians.

On the 16th of September the residents of Tucson celebrated Mexican Independence day. The Urias family has recalled that this was one

Viola Terrazas dressed in traditional Sonoran costume for Mexican Independence Day.   *1939*
P͟H͟O͟T͟O͟ ͟C͟O͟U͟R͟T͟E͟S͟Y͟ ͟O͟F͟ ͟V͟I͟O͟L͟A͟ ͟T͟E͟R͟R͟A͟Z͟A͟S͟

of the most widely celebrated days in Tucson when they were children. The *Junta Patriótica* and the *Alianza Hispano-Americana* were very active in promoting the welfare of Mexican-Americans. They hosted this annual celebration with a parade. The young women of Tucson sold tickets to the celebration. The person who sold the most tickets became the queen of the parade and rode in a special coach. The parade started on Main and went east on Congress to 6th Avenue and then to Armory Park. There was a patriotic program with speeches, songs, and dances. A free barbecue was held in the park. [5] This was a very special celebration for the Mexican-American people of Tucson.

On the cover of Thomas Sheridan's book, *Los Tucsonenses*, there is a photograph of a young woman wearing a hat and sash. That photograph actually is of one of the queens of the Mexican Independence Day parade. The Urias and Terrazas cousins were surprised and upset that it was not acknowledged as such but rather described as a Fourth of July photo. They remembered the young woman and it brought back memories of the selection process for the queen.

The other thing the Urias sisters remembered was that Ignacia Urias made candies, *cubiertos de calabaza* and *visnaga*, that she sold to people who had gathered at Armory Park. As people strolled through the park there were many vendors selling food and treats. It was an easy way for Ignacia to make pocket money by doing something she enjoyed. Cubiertas de calabaza were made with pumpkin and panocha. Visnaga is made from the pulp of the barrel cactus. The pulp was cured in lime-water, washed and rinsed well, then boiled with sugar syrup until it reached the correct consistency. It was a yellow color and a soft consistency with a granulated crust. It is also known as cactus candy.

Armistice Day (now called Veteran's Day) was always celebrated on November 11. Ignacia Urias made new dresses for her daughters because children from the schools participated in a parade. Prizes were given for the best marching units. Church bells were rung to mark the hour at which the World War I armistice had been signed. The school children marched by grades and they had to practice marching and lining up correctly. A trophy was given to the school with the best marching group. Veterans also marched in the parade. There was a large truck that carried veterans who were disabled or mentally affected by the traumas they had experienced. Their appearances and utterances were frightening to many children. The parade took place in the morning and was over whenever the parade arrived at Armory Park, usually by noon.[6] Celia Diaz was actually able to remember the end of World War I. She recalled that she was frightened because all the bells in the city, including those at fire stations, were rung and people rushed out of their homes rejoicing at the end of the war. Celia stated that Armistice Day was one of her earliest memories and that was why it was so important to her.

El Día de los Muertos (All Souls' Day) was an important Catholic holy day that was celebrated in a very Mexican way. Typically families attended mass together. After mass the people went to Holy Hope cemetery, which at that time was the northwest border of Tucson. Families manicured the graves of departed relatives and decorated them with flowers. The Papago Indians would arrive by wagon and leave food on their gravesites. This was a much-discussed custom among the children. They were allowed to watch, but were never to interfere with or question the Indians. Some people would take the spirit of the day to the extreme and cry and carry on. Members of the Urias family remembered that there had been a man who had lived on Congress and was not well liked within the Mexican-American community. When he died his wife threw herself on the grave and carried on; this behavior continued every Día de los Muertos. As children, it was an exciting spectacle to watch.[2]

Maria Muñoz felt that el Día do los Muertos was an especially significant day. Their Tío Alejandro Bernal (married to Angela Terrazas) would send Ignacia Urias large, white pompom chrysanthemums to be distributed on the graves of the deceased relatives. The Bernal family lived in Los Angeles and had the flowers shipped to Tucson. They were primarily for Ygnacio, Brígida, and Altagracia Terrazas. The arrival of the flowers at the Urias home on 6th Avenue was very exciting for the whole family. They were brought in a truck-like railroad wagon drawn by a horse. As time went by this progressed to a small open truck without a roof. The flowers arrived one to two days before All Souls' Day. Ignacia would put the flowers in the bathtub and fill it with water. When el Día de los Muertos arrived the extended Terrazas family went to Holy Hope Cemetery to clean the plots and place flowers on the graves of their grandparents and Altagracia.

Thanksgiving was celebrated in Tucson as in the rest of the country. I used to ask my mother what they ate that day and she always laughed and told us it was the same thing everyone else ate, turkey. The children learned the story of Thanksgiving at school. The Urias family had a very humorous anecdote about this holiday. The Hayman Krupp Company would send the family a live turkey in a crate, which was shipped from El Paso by train and then delivered by a truck. One year young Ignacio Urias was in charge of killing the turkey but it got away from him. The turkey jumped over the backyard fence and ran down Stone Avenue. The whole neighborhood gave chase until the turkey was captured.

Killing the turkey was another story. Since the turkey was larger than a chicken (which was usually killed by wringing its neck) it had to be dispatched by a different method. On the third step down from the back porch a stone was laid. Normally Gilberto would hold the bird's head down on the stone and Gonzalo would hit it on the neck with an ax to sever the head. The body would immediately be placed in a tub of boiling water for a few seconds so that the feathers could be pulled off easily. Thanksgiving dinner in Tucson was similar to those in the rest of the country. The turkey was stuffed with dressing, they had potatoes, and, of course, they had pumpkin pie. This was a meal that was usually enjoyed with immediate family and later in the afternoon they would visit the homes of extended family or friends.

The other events that were always celebrated by families were *cumpleaños* (birthdays). Bertha Terrazas remembered that each person would choose a special birthday meal. Her special meal was fried chicken and I remember my mother saying that her special meal was enchiladas sonorenses. They then had a cake. In the Terrazas family the children were given useful gifts. It was something they needed, usually clothes. The girls were each given a ring on their twelfth birthday.[8] My mother gave me her ring on my fourteenth birthday (she feared that I would lose it so the ring was given to me two years later than was her family tradition). It is something I wear to this day.

The Urias family often celebrated several birthdays together. Piñatas filled with candy were used for each party. They usually had strawberry shortcake and ice cream. When the birthday person woke in the morning they were serenaded with the song, "Las Mañanitas." The Urias daughters also received rings on their twelfth birthday. It was not necessarily on the exact day, but when their father returned from a sales trip.[9]

The one birthday that was specifically observed was that of Ignacia Urias. Her family and close friends would visit bringing her bouquets of her favorite flowers, *azucenas* and *San Miguelito* (tuberoses and Queen's Wreath). Ignacia would prepare refreshments to serve her guests. She

Amalia Terrazas.   *c. 1921*

usually had teswin or tepache de piña and dozens of bizcochuelos.[10] It is interesting to note that she made her own refreshments so this was really not a day of rest for her, but rather one to spend entertaining family and friends.

---

1   Muñoz interview, 3 May 1997.

2   Ibid.

3   *Arizona Daily Star*, 19 April 1930.

4   Sheridan, *Los Tucsonenses*, 161.

5   Muñoz interview, 3 May 1997.

6   Ibid.

7   McCauslin, Terrazas Family History, 2.

8   Ibid.

9   Muñoz interview, 3 May 1997.

10   Ibid.

CHAPTER 10

Family Outings

Como me gusta lo bueno, me quadra lo regular.

WHEN MY MOTHER was a child the trolley line went past her home on South Stone Avenue. The family fondly remembered the trolley cars and the places they were able to go on the line. As a child I was fascinated by the fact that something so wonderful had been paved over in the name of progress. For my mother's family the trolleys held many memories of family outings. My mother and her extended family loved telling stories of the special things they remembered about Tucson. These were very vivid memories of enjoyable places and fun activities. It was difficult for us, as children, to visualize their Tucson because so many things had changed after World War II. Tucson had become a large city as opposed to the sleepy, dusty town they had known.

Tucson had an interesting public transportation system. Originally James Buell was the driving force behind the Tucson Land and Herdic Coach Company. He traveled to Philadelphia in September 1881 to meet Peter Herdic, designer of the Herdic coach. One or two mules drew Herdic coaches; they were enclosed, had a back entrance, and parallel rows of side seats. Buell paid $500 for the rights to build and operate Herdic coaches in Tucson. The first coach was delivered November 16, 1881, and went into service before the company was incorporated.[1] The coaches ran between 6 A.M. and 9 P.M. Tickets were sold by the drivers and by Williams Scott's insurance company at the corner of Meyer Street and Maiden Lane.[2] The coaches probably operated until beyond 1888, but it is unclear when they were discontinued. No long-term transit service operated between then and fall of 1897.

The chief promoter of the Tucson Street Railway was Charles Hoff.

The company was organized in September 1897. It used mule-drawn cars until June 1906. Then electric streetcars went into operation and the name became TRT or Tucson Rapid Transit. Both the mule-drawn cars and the later electric cars provided transportation from Congress Street and Stone Avenue to the university campus and on to Elysian Grove via South Stone Avenue and 17th Street. As the city expanded so did the routes of the TRT. There were two main loops, one for the downtown area and one to the university. Later the TRT had two other streetcar franchises (which it didn't operate). One ran north from Stone to Speedway and then to Grant Road and Oracle Road. (At that time Grant was called Luna and Oracle was called 12th Avenue.) The other ran from 4th and Toole Avenue forming a loop of 9th Street, 5th, 1st, and Park Avenues, north to Speedway Boulevard, then east to the city boundary at Olsen. Around 1912 the Main Avenue line, another route to the university, was put in service.

These electric cars, known as trolleys, were a popular means of transportation and provided great amusement for the Tucson citizens. The trolleys were quite colorful – they were painted green and yellow – and could carry thirty seated passengers. The fare was eight cents one way and fifteen cents for round trip. The trolley cars shortened the amount of time it took university students to get to their primary area of entertainment, Elysian Grove. The trolleys themselves were also an amusement for university students and were the object of many pranks, such as greasing the wheels or actually being removed from the tracks. They also linked the people of Tucson to activities that took place at the University of Arizona.[3]

Amalia Terrazas often talked of taking the streetcars downtown. Celia Diaz recalled that her family would often take them to the University of Arizona for family outings. Lupe Urias remembered that one of the lines ran on 17th and that it was quite a treat to ride on the cars. The University of Arizona was a special destination because the children would go look at the aviary and walk around the campus.[4]

The Aviary, also called the Bird Cage, was in use from 1918 to 1939. Initially it was located just inside the Main Gate at 3rd Street and Park Avenue. The Aviary was built with a $1,700 donation, probably from Mrs. Lavinia Steward. The aviary was meant to house birds that represented southern Arizona. By the end of 1919 it housed owls, hawks, doves, several varieties of parrots, and an eagle. The aviary had three successive homes on the University campus. It was unpopular with University students and the noise made it unpopular with neighboring residents. In 1924 the Aviary was moved to the far northeast side of campus near the power plant. The Urias family recalled that they visited the aviary when it was by the power plant. From 1936 to 1938 it was moved to the corner of Highland Avenue and 4th Street. Finally, in 1939, the University donated the aviary to the Pima County Park Commission for a wildlife project in the Tucson Mountains.[5] Although it may have been a nuisance to neighborhood residents and unpopular with students, it was enchanting to the Urias and Terrazas children and it remained a fond memory.

Aside from the Aviary, the university campus was also an attraction. It had broad green malls that were meticulously landscaped. There was

The Terrazas and Urias families often took trolleys to go downtown or to the University of Arizona.   *c. 1920s*

an extensive cactus garden and a nursery was kept to supply the plants needed to maintain the grounds. All of the buildings on campus were constructed of red brick and seemed quite elegant to the visiting children. It was a place of dreams for them.

As previously mentioned, the University of Arizona hosted the city's Fourth of July celebrations for many years. This practice began in the mid-1920s. The public was invited to attend the festivities at the campus athletic field at 7:30 P.M. The band played, a patriotic address was given, there were games, and finally a huge fireworks display was put on. The celebrations varied somewhat each year but seemed to be consistently sponsored by the Junior Chamber of Commerce.[6]

After these excursions the tired and moonstruck children would be shepherded back to the streetcars for the short ride home. It was with great disappointment on their part that the trolleys were discontinued. They never understood why the service was ended and complained that it was the most reliable source of transportation available to them at the time. Some today might argue that they were correct.

The electric cars had provided a great service for the city of Tucson. But by the late 1920s people began to complain about the interference of the trolleys with automobile traffic. In early 1930 the city council requested advice on whether to continue the streetcar system and the answer was "No." The last trolley cars ran until January 1, 1931, when they were discontinued and replaced by buses.

The only remnants of the streetcar system are the rails. Most of them are covered by asphalt, but in heavily trafficked areas the asphalt has worn through and the tracks are visible.[7] These rails were very obvious to my siblings and cousins as we made visits to our grandparents' home on South Stone Avenue. We frequently wondered why the trolleys had been discontinued as the stories we had been told certainly indicated that they had been useful. But not only that, they had provided wonderful pastimes for the citizens of Tucson. It was apparent to me that my mother was extremely disappointed when the colorful trolleys were removed from service.

One of my family's favorite Sunday activities was a car ride around the outskirts of town. At least, it was my mother's favorite activity because she was the one who took us on these outings. She told us that Francisco Terrazas would bundle his children into their small Ford truck, which they called the Foringo, for similar drives. We used to imagine that when she was a child these drives must have been extremely far from their home. As she drove she would point out different sites and tell us a brief history about each of them. Some of them had changed, some of them no longer existed, but we were able to imagine them as she had seen them as a child.

One of our favorite drives was to go east on Fort Lowell Road. First of all, this was only three blocks north of our home. Our destination was to see the cemetery by old Fort Lowell. We never stopped – a chain-link fence enclosed the cemetery. My mother told us her family had never stopped as that would have been disrespectful to the dead and their families. We were lead to believe that most of those buried there were American Indians and soldiers from the fort. We believed this cemetery to be ancient and were fearful that there were many ghosts in the area. Indeed, my mother told us that several of her friends had seen unusual apparitions in that area at night. It was not a place to be after dark.

I have since learned that this cemetery is known as the Cemetery of *El Fuerte*. In 1891 the U.S. government abandoned the Fort Lowell site. A group of Mexican-American residents began occupying the areas around the fort. This became known as the El Fuerte community and was primarily agricultural. By the late 1940s much of the community was incorporated into the ever-expanding city of Tucson. The people buried in the Cemetery of El Fuerte were in fact residents of this small Mexican-American enclave. The cemetery was originally part of a ranch owned by Melville Haskell and later purchased by the Porter family. There was an unwritten agreement between Mr. Haskell and Mr. Porter that the small plot – it was less than one acre – would always remain a cemetery.[8] In 1926 Pima County established the area around Fort Lowell as a historic district.

Our next destination was River Road where we made a loop from Fort Lowell Road to Swan Road and then west on River Road. My mother told us that this road had also existed in her day and ran parallel to the Rillito River. As I recall, the land in this area seemed a little greener than the desert on either side. Or maybe it was my mother's stories: her family had enjoyed this part of their drive because it was always a little cooler and greener. She told us that originally there had been cattle ranches in the area but later people had raised horses there. She and her siblings had loved to look at the animals. She said there had also been large cottonwoods along the river. The road always appeared more shady and inviting than the desert, which she said was a welcome relief.

River Road itself was full of dips and she said her father would drive a little faster so that the dips and bumps would give the children butterflies in their stomachs. She described it as a bit like a roller coaster. But when they wanted an even bigger thrill they would ask their father to take them to Roller Coaster Road. I imagine that this truly was a long drive from their home as it was quite a drive from our home when I was young. We too were taken along this road and experienced the same elation that my mother had experienced as a child.

After the family drives Francisco Terrazas took the children for ice cream. Their destination before going home was the Palace of Sweets. There were two shops, one at 1 West Congress and the other at 125 East Congress. Minos and Nick Vakares owned the Palace of Sweets. These brothers were Greek immigrants who felt there was a need in the town

La Tiendita de Gallegos.   *1996*
PHOTO FROM THE AUTHOR'S COLLECTION

for a confection shop. It was from visiting these shops that the Terrazas and Urias children developed their sweet tooth. The shop they primarily remember was the one on East Congress. Viola Terrazas remembered that the Palace of Sweets had a soda fountain and lots of chocolates.[9] Here they would purchase their ice cream cones after their Sunday afternoon outings. There were also cactus candy, root beer floats, and sundaes of different varieties.[10] It was just fun for the children to look at the different items in the shop. My mother recalled that in those days it was possible to purchase an ice cream cone for a nickel and a large Tootsie Roll for a penny. Next to the Lyric Theater was Sam's Place, which the Terrazas children graduated to after they had outgrown the Palace of Sweets. They were able to get hamburgers, hot lunches, and cokes.

The other treat was walking to la Tiendita de Gallego on Meyer and 17th. *Cimarronas,* also called *raspados*, were sold in this tiny neighborhood market. Cimarronas were flavored shaved ice. Especially popular were strawberry, pineapple, and *leche* (condensed milk). In the summer the children would walk to this store. Groups of children would stand in line to buy cimarronas. The eldest Terrazas sisters were expected to take the rest of the children. The cimarronas cost a nickel and the children were allowed to go to the window and order their desired flavor.[11] In 1996 I accompanied my aunt Viola on a sightseeing tour of her neighborhood. The Tiendita de Gallego was still standing although its windows were boarded. My aunt said that the building brought back many fond memories.

My mother always told us that she never remembered that Tucson was as hot when she was young as it was when we grew up. She felt that all of the buildings and asphalt streets of the city held in the heat. I was never quite sure that this was true. But even so, in her day it was still hot enough for the children to want to be in the water. When I was growing up in Tucson during the 1950s and 60s the only time water ran in the riverbeds was during the rainy season. My mother said that when she had been a child there was usually water running in the Santa Cruz year-round, even if it was only a small trickle.

Before 1880 the Santa Cruz River did indeed have water flowing year-round, although the amount was dependent on the season.[12] Starting in the 1850s farmers and businessmen began to use this water for irrigation. Because of irrigation practices, the water tables dropped and the amount of water flowing in the Santa Cruz was decreased significantly. By the early 1900s the amount of water in the river was dependent on the seasonal rainfalls.

Both the Urias and Terrazas families liked to go on picnics. They almost always went to the Santa Cruz River during the summer rainy season. There was a dam on The Santa Cruz near San Xavier that formed a good-sized swimming hole.[13] I think this swimming hole was what became known as Silver Lake. The children were allowed to "swim" in the river in their underwear. As they got older the girls had to wear bathing costumes, which consisted of midi-shirts and bloomers (as my mother described them). My mother had several pictures of children swimming in the river, but the water level couldn't have been more than five inches. I think they primarily splashed about in the muddy water. Ignacia Urias and Virginia Terrazas occasionally entered the water to cool off but they spent most of their time supervising from the shade of the cottonwoods.

Other areas were also popular for swimming and picnicking but were quite a drive. Patagonia, Sabino Canyon, and the Molina ranch on the banks of the San Pedro River were other favored spots. The most popular day to go to the swimming areas was the Día de San Juan. The children were told that wading in the water took their sins away.[14] Besides the usual picnic lunch of sandwiches, the Terrazas and Urias families always had a large watermelon, which was a special treat.

Tucson also had several public swimming pools. The most popular was Wetmore pool, which was located at 309 East Wetmore (a half-mile east of Oracle). The pool was in operation from 1918 to 1974.[15] Edward Wetmore Jr. built the pool after seeing community children swim in a ditch containing well water. The pool was part of Wetmore Amusement Park. At its height the park included outdoor movies, a roller rink, and a dance pavilion.[16] It was a special treat for the Urias and Terrazas children to go to Wetmore Park. They enjoyed the pool and roller rink. As they became older the dance pavilion was also an attraction. My mother was terrified of swimming because she said she had almost drowned in Wetmore pool. She was never allowed to take swimming lessons because it was a luxury her family couldn't afford. She said she preferred to sit at the edge of the pool or stay in the shallow end.

However, as afraid as she was of swimming, Wetmore Park was a welcome oasis during the sweltering summers.

An activity that I had never heard of from my mother, but which her Urias cousins discussed, was to go *bellotear* (to gather acorns). The family would gather acorns that had fallen on the ground. Their favorite spots to gather belloteas were the foothills near Benson, Oracle, or Patagonia. The acorns were gathered, cracked, and mixed with jellybeans and provided a great treat.[17] Needless to say, they weren't a treat that lasted very long.

A Mountain had long been known in Tucson as Sentinel Peak. On November 6, 1915, the U of A football team scored a victory over Pomona College. Civil engineering student Albert Condron suggested that an A be placed on the peak to commemorate the victory. He surveyed the area and construction was started one week later. Students and loyal town fans constructed the A. It was whitewashed on March 4, 1916.[18] Since that day the peak has been called A Mountain. It continues to be an annual event for U of A students to repaint the A white.

A Mountain was an enjoyable car ride for the Terrazas and Urias children. Once they arrived at the top they could survey the city. Family excursions to A Mountain were usually seasonal and often had an additional purpose to being an amusement for the children. In the spring they would climb up A Mountain to dig *covenas*. The covena is a bulbous desert plant with a flower that resembles a bluebell. Once the plants were uprooted, the flowers were gathered and taken home. The bulbs were eaten raw and considered a delicacy.[19] In June fruit from the saguaros was gathered to make jelly and candy. The children helped use long poles to obtain the fruit. Before Christmas they would gather mistletoe from various trees to hang above doorways.

Although Tucson was a relatively small city in the early 1900s, families were able to find a variety of entertaining activities. Many of their jaunts were for relaxation, but often the adults were able to use them for purposeful activities as well; time was not to be wasted. Work activities were often meshed with fun outings for the children. They provided many memorable occasions for the Terrazas and Urias families as well as for countless other families in Tucson.

1   Haney and Scavone, "Cars Stop Here," 47.

2   Caywood, *A History of Tucson Transportation*, 20.

3   Haney and Scavone, "Cars Stop Here," 51, 55–56, 61.

4   McCauslin, Terrazas Family History, 1.

5   Ball, *Photographic History*, 115, 160–161, 432–433; Martin, Douglas. *The Lamp in the Desert: The Story of the University of Arizona* (Tucson: University of Arizona Press, 1960), 137–138.

6   *Tucson Daily Citizen*, 3 July 1930.

7   Haney and Scavone, "Cars Stop Here," 63.

8   Davenport, Michal. "Arizona Historic Landscapes Focusing on Evergreen Cemetery and Memorial Park, Holy Hope Cemetery, The Cemetery of "El Fuerte", and the Rincon Memorial Cemetery." (paper presented to University of Arizona Landscape Architecture Program, Tucson, November 1995), 12.

9   Viola Terrazas, interview by author, 22 August 1996.

10 *Arizona Daily Star*, 26 May 1954.

11 Terrazas interview, 22 August 1996.

12 Sheridan, *Los Tucsonenses*, 63.

13 Muñoz interview, 3 May 1997.

14 McCauslin, Family History, 1.

15 Bonnie Henry, *Arizona Daily Star*, 2 June 1974.

16 Deborah Block, "Old Pueblo: Six Decades of Exciting Living in Tucson," *Tucson Daily Citizen* (8 March 1979): 5.

17 Muñoz interview, 3 May 1997.

18 Ball, *Photographic History*, 108.

19 Muñoz interview, 3 May 1997.

CHAPTER *II*

Games

Naranja dulce, limón partido.

FOR CHILDREN growing up in the 1920s and 1930s Tucson was a fairly safe place. Looking back on life in Tucson during their childhoods, both the Urias and Terrazas cousins recalled that Tucson was a small, peaceful, and happy town. They also remembered it as being quite dusty. Most children were allowed to have a certain amount of freedom around their neighborhoods. People were on a first name basis.

The cousins didn't recall that their neighborhood, which was east of South Stone, was called by any particular name. They were allowed to go east of South Stone, but needed special permission to go to the west of this street. They were also allowed to go north to the downtown area. In order to get there the children relied on their roller skates. Roller skates were a precious commodity and guarded by their owners. The skates were made larger or smaller using a skate key, which was worn around the skater's neck on a string. This is how the skates were put on or taken off the skater's shoes. Initially the children would skate round and round the block from the Terrazas home to the Urias home. However, as they became bolder they often skated to the downtown area and back, enjoying any hill or slope in the sidewalk.

By this point the children were older and more aware of social differences in Tucson. They recalled that there were a few wealthy people in their neighborhood, including the author Harold Bell Wright. Mr. Wright would yell at the children if they were making too much noise on their skates. They were not allowed to go to Barrio Anita unless accompanied by an adult. Anglos who were in a different socioeconomic class started moving north and east of Tucson. Another area that was off limits was Paseo Redondo, where the wealthy merchant class lived. Blacks were segregated in an area south of Congress between Main and Stone and primarily on Meyer and Convent Streets.[1] Although the Urias and Terrazas cousins say they were not aware of discrimination toward Mexican-Americans, they rarely socialized with the Anglo population.

During the early part of the 1900s children's play was very active and imaginative. They played childhood favorites such as tag, hide-and-seek, and London Bridge. However, they also played games that were

Top to bottom: Maria Luisa, Bertha, Delia, Zarina, Amalia, Fresia Terrazas.   *c. 1925*
PHOTO COURTESY OF VIOLA TERRAZAS

part of their cultural heritage. These are games that I fear may be lost to future generations. My cousins who are a decade older than I remember some of these games, but they were something that I never learned. I think it is imperative that they be recorded or they will be completely forgotten. In our computerized age children simply don't play these types of games – television and computers have replaced them.

There were several hide-and-seek or tag-type games that were very popular. The first is called *las calabacitas*, which was a tag game similar to "duck, duck, gray duck." Children gathered in a circle and the person who was "it" went around and hugged each of the others. The person who wasn't hugged became "it." It had a verse that was recited: "Las calabacitas, se queman, se queman los que no se abrazan." The translation for this verse is, "The little squash are burning, are burning, those that aren't burned are hugged."

Another favorite was *Ron Chi Flan* (run sheep run). In this game the children extended the limits of their territory beyond the block on which they lived. Ron Chi Flan was played with two groups. One group ran and hid, leaving one child to draw a map telling where the group was located. The other group then had to find them. If the first group reached home base, they were safe.

Naranja Dulce was a game similar to London Bridge. The children formed a circle by holding hands leaving someone in the center and sing a song, which went:

Naranja dulce, limón partido	Sweet orange, tart lemon
Dáme un abrazo	Give me a hug
Por Dios te pido.	I ask from God.
La marcha toca	The march plays
Mi pecho llora	My heart cries
Adios señora	Goodbye my lady
Yo ya me voy.	I'm going now.
Si fueron falsos	If they were false
Sus juramentos	Your promises (statements)
En algún tiempo	At some time
Te voy a olvidar.	I'll forget you.

When the song had ended the child in the center chose who they wanted a hug from. That person would then go into the center and the other person would go out. And so the game would continue.

Agua y té (also called *Matarile*) was very popular and also similar to London Bridge.

Agua y té	Water and tea
Matarile rile rile	Matarile rile rile
Agua y té	Water and tea
Matarile rile ron.	Matarile rile ron.
Escógalo usted	You choose him/her
Matarile rile rile	Matarile rile rile
Escógalo usted	You choose him/her
Matarile rile ron.	Matarile rile ron.
Escogo a (person's name)	I choose (person's name)
Matarile rile rile	Matarile rile rile
Escogo a (person's name)	I choose (person's name)
Matarile rile ron.	Matarile rile ron.
Aquí entrego a mi hijo/a	Here I send my son/daughter
Con dolor de corazón	With pain in my heart
Matarile rile rile	Matarile rile rile
Aquí entrego a mi hijo/a	Here I send my son/daughter
Con dolor de corazón	With pain in my heart
Matarile rile ron.	Matarile rile ron.

Other verses might include the following:

¿Quién quiere usted?	Who do you want?
Matarile rile rile	Matarile rile rile
¿Quién quiere usted?	Who do you want?
Matarile rile ron	Matarile rile ron
Quiero a un/a marquís/a	I want a marques/marquesa
Matarile rile rile	Matarile rile rile
Quiere un/a marquís/a	I want a marques/marquesa
Matarile rile ron.	Matarile rile ron.

This game has an interesting history. In some places it is called Ambo Gato. The game can be traced to a French song, "Ah Mon Beau Chateau." The nonsense line in French was originally "Ma tante, tire, lire, lire." The lyrics in Spanish come from a mistranslation of French.[2] Many of my cousins recall playing this game, but I don't and our children didn't play it either.

Many shorter games were played with very young toddlers and babies. Older children were encouraged to help their mothers by playing with younger siblings. The Terrazas and Urias cousins fondly remembered these games. In fact, I remember many of these and sang them to my children. Many of these songs have their origins in Tucson.[3]

"Reque" is a song sung while rocking a baby back and forth:

Reque reque reque ran.	Reque reque reque ran.
La madera de San Juan.	The wood of St. John.
Pide pan y no le dan.	He asks for bread and they wouldn't give it to him.
Pide queso y le dan un hueso.	He asks for cheese and is given a bone.
Y le troza el pescuezo.	And his neck is broken.

(The following line can be interchanged with the above.)

Que se le atora en el pescuezo.	Which sticks in his throat.

When the song is finished you tickle the baby or giggle to make him or her laugh. I loved this song as a child, but I never understood why it was so macabre.

"Lulú que Lulú" is also sung while rocking a baby.

Lulú que lulú que San Camaleón	Lulu que lulu que San Camaleon
Debajo de un hueco	Underneath a bone
Salió un ratón	Went a rat
Mátalo, mátalo por ladrón.	Kill it, kill it, it's a thief.
Éste niño quiere	This child wants
Que le cante yo	Me to sing to him
Una cancioncita	A little song
Que me lo parió.	Since I gave birth to him.

I remember listening to my mother sing this song to my sister and brothers when I was quite young. She sang with much love and affection. It was something I learned and in turn sang it to my children as I rocked them to sleep. Again, portions of this song are a little gruesome, but I hope it will be passed on through the generations.

Hace La Mosita is a game played with toddlers. While tapping them on the head you say:

Hace la mosita	Make a little fist and tap
En la cabecita.	On the little head.
Con la piedra grande	With a big rock
Y la más chiquita.	And a smaller one.
Sas, sas, sas	Tap, tap, tap
En la cabecita.	On the little head.

I remember this song with great fondness. One of my most treasured memories is of my mother playing this game with my son, Matthew. It is special to me because she developed Alzheimer's disease shortly afterwards and was unable to sing this to my daughter, Megan.

Tortillitas is a game played like pat-a-cake:

Tortillitas para mamá.	Tortillitas for mama.
Tortillitas para papá.	Tortillitas for papa.
Tortillitas para su mami.	Tortillitas for your mami.
Tortillitas para su papi.	Tortillitas for your papi.
Tortillitas para su hermana.	Tortillitas for your sister.
Tortillitas para su hermano.	Tortillitas for your brother.

Again, this is a game I can recall my mother playing with my siblings and also with my son.

I do not recall that my mother played the following games with us. However, many of my cousins remembered them. My aunts Zarina and Bertha sang them to their children. My cousins related them to me.

Pon, Pon, Pon is a pointing game. The palm of one hand is extended and the index finger of the other hand is tapped on it while saying:

Pon, pon, pon	Pon, pon, pon
El dedito en el buzón.	The little finger in the mailbox.

Mano a la Negra is another game similar to pat-a-cake:

Que se le cáe la mano a la negra	The black woman's hand is falling.
Y no se le quiebra	And it doesn't break
Tiene manita	She has a little hand
No tiene manita	She doesn't have a little hand
Porque la tiene desconchifladita.	Because it is not working.

I have to admit that this verse doesn't make much sense to me and I can't imagine where it came from. My cousins recalled that it was a very old verse.

Last but not least are the *dichos* (sayings) that we learned. Or, should I say we constantly heard? These dichos are bittersweet memories for me. Although humorous, they were always said with a lesson in mind. Viola Terrazas and I spent an afternoon recalling the dichos said most often in our family.

Dime con quién andas y te dire quién eres.
(Tell me who you go with and I'll tell you who you are.)

Ay, que gente dejó Juarez.
(Oh, what people Juarez left.)

Ay, me lleva el tren.
(I lost my train of thought.)

Mejor sola que mal acompañada.
(You're better off alone than in the wrong company.)

En boca cerrada no entran moscas.
(A closed mouth catches no flies. Think before you speak.)

Si no tienes nada bueno que decir, mejor no digas nada.
(If you don't have anything good to say, it's better to say nothing.)

Cáe más pronto un hablador que un cojo.
(A gossip is usually the first to fall.)

No hay mal que por bien no venga.
(There's no evil that does not bring some good.)

No más entran como burros sin mecate.
(Don't come barging in like a donkey without a load.)

Más vale tarde que nunca.
(Better late than never.)

El golpe avisa.
(You'll know it when it happens.)

Lo que se siembra se recoge.
(You reap what you sow.)

No me hagas la vida pesada.
(Don't make things difficult for me.)

Me cáe pesada.
(It rubs me the wrong way.)

Como me gusta lo bueno, me cuadra lo regular.
(I like the best, but if I can't have it, I'll settle for next best.)

No seas tan mula.
(Don't be so stubborn.)

Panza llena, corazón contento.
(Full stomach, contented heart.)

Querer es poder.
(If you want something bad enough, you'll get it.)

Querer y sin ganas.
(Where there's a will there's a way.)

Ya estoy arta de todo esto.
(I'm fed up with all of this.)

Ay, que vida tan chucha.
(What a dog's life.)

Mi casa es su casa.
(My house is your house.)

Ánimo y arriba los corazones.
(Courage and onward the hearts.)

My cousins and I agreed that the dicho that had the most impact on us was "Dime con quién andas y te dire quién eres." This was especially appropriate during adolescence and provoked a great deal of anger when pronounced by our parents. We hated to admit that we now realized why our mothers said this. But in retrospect, we felt that this dicho was quite relevant, truthful, and was one of our favorites. It is the dicho most used by our family currently.

———•••———

1   Muñoz interview, 3 May 1997.

2   West, John. *Mexican-American Folklore* (Little Rock, Ark.: August House Publishers, 1988), 192.

3   Ibid., 54.

CHAPTER 12

Ghost Stories

El golpe avisa.

MEXICAN PEOPLE are very superstitious and have great belief in ghosts. They have premonitions and portents of doom. They believe in spirits and wandering souls. Ghost stories abound in the barrios of Tucson. Most of the stories I heard were stories that have been handed down in our family. Again, most of these stories have a moral and are told to teach a lesson. It is believed that if you allow yourself you will at some time in your life see ghosts. My mother told me that it is common to see or dream of ghosts. Usually this spirit or soul appears because it desires prayers, wants to comfort the family member, or has a message to deliver. When my mother died I felt certain that she would appear to me, but I never saw her. One of my cousins told me it was because I was not ready to see her. She said that when I allowed myself to experience this, my mother would appear. This belief in spirits is something I inherited from my family.

Before the advent of television and computers, and especially during summer thunderstorms, families would gather to tell ghost stories. As a child Lupe Urias had the reputation of being quite proficient in telling ghost stories. She, however, denied this and said that she couldn't remember being any better than her siblings or cousins in this regard. However, her Terrazas cousins remembered her as a champion teller of ghost tales.

There were several givens about superstitions in Tucson. The howling wind sounds like a crying woman and spirits are likely to be wandering during windstorms. Summer thunderstorms with their spectacular lightening displays are frequently noted for spirit activity. A hooting owl or a howling dog are omens of impending death and hovering ghosts. These, then, become the perfect times for telling ghost stories.

I can also recall my mother telling me that there were certain people or families within the community that were psychic. These families had the ability to see ghosts or communicate messages from spirits. The family with whom she was most familiar was the Navarro family. They lived on the west side of South Stone Avenue. (Members of the Navarro family continue to live in that home.)

The most famous ghost story in the barrio district is that of *La Llorona* (the crying woman). My mother told us this story during thunderstorms. It was said that in the early days of Tucson a woman threw several of her children into the Santa Cruz River. After she died her ghost wondered up and down the riverbanks at night crying for the lost children. We were told that when my mother was young she was told that she must never go near the banks of the river in the evening. If you did, you would risk meeting La Llorona. Of course, we were told this tale to keep us from wandering at night. This is actually quite an old tale and has many variations based on the town in which it's told. It is a familiar theme in Mexico and Central America.[1]

El Tiradito (the Wishing Shrine) is located on South Main Street near the intersection of Cushing. In the Urias and Terrazas families the story that was handed down was that of a young, married woman. She had a *novio* (boyfriend) whom her husband discovered. Her husband killed the novio with a knife during a brawl. His mother built the shrine in his honor. People would take candles to the site, say a prayer, and hope that their prayers would be answered. Although this was a site that could be visited during the day, one was not to be near it at night. It was said that the young man's mother could be heard weeping for him at night. My mother said that she thought she had once heard her sobs when walking in that neighborhood one evening. She felt that she shouldn't be there again after it was dark.

Another story my mother liked to tell my sister and me was that of the handsome stranger and the dance. She assured us that this was a Tucson folktale that she had heard from her parents. It happened that dances were held in La Placita during her grandparents' day. A young woman wanted to go to the dance, but her father wouldn't permit her attendance. She managed to sneak out of the house unattended by a

El Tiradito.   *1996*

chaperone. While at the dance she met a very handsome stranger. The two of them proceeded to dance together that evening. When her father discovered that she was gone, he went to the dance to retrieve her. She was, of course, very embarrassed and didn't want to leave, but her father insisted. The stranger was very angry and continued to dance with the young woman while her father pleaded with her to leave. As the dancing continued the crowd and the father noticed that the stranger's feet became the cloven feet of a goat. Finally, he disappeared in a cloud of sulfuric smoke. The stranger was, in fact, a devil. The moral of the story was that children shouldn't be disobedient to their parents or they would have to suffer the consequences.

One of the most beautiful areas outside Tucson is Gate's Pass. I loved to go there but my mother said she wasn't fond of it because of a ghost story she had heard as a child. She was told that there was a stage robber who took gold from the Butterfield Stage Lines and hid his cache in a cave by Gate's Pass. He was killed one day but his ghost and that of his horse still guarded the cave where the money was hidden. Many people had searched for the gold but the robber and his horse protected the cave. My mother told us that many people had searched for the gold and that a sign of ghostly treasure was a glowing blue light. Treasure seekers would be able to follow this blue light to the treasure chest of gold. But because of the fierce bandit and his horse, this treasure had never been found. There are many caves in the Gate's Pass area, but my mother warned us that they were not to be explored unless one wanted to risk their life.

My Aunt Viola walked me past a building on the 400 block of South Stone that is said to be haunted. This adobe building has been haunted for many years and she and her siblings were aware of it when they were younger. During the day they would skate by the building but would never go near it after dark. My aunt said that an old man haunted the building but she had never seen the ghost. The building is still there and to this day people avoid walking past that area when it is dark.

According to my mother, the Navarro family home on South Stone was also haunted. It frightened me to know that my mother had been in the home. She said that she had never seen ghosts in that home and was not afraid to visit the family. She said that the Navarro family had the ability to see ghosts and members of that family did not fear them. The

Navarros and the ghosts in the home lived in harmony with each other. The ghosts were not there to harm the family; they simply shared the home with each other. In fact, the Navarros still live in that home, which is down the block from my grandmother's house.

An incident that my mother and the Terrazas family were involved in related to a young woman named Norma Moore who was from southern Arizona (the Douglas or Agua Prieta area). Strange things happened to this young woman, and people thought she was possessed by the devil. She was taken to priests in Douglas but they were unable to help her so she was taken to Tucson. Aunt Viola believed that Norma Moore arrived in Tucson around 1937. For some reason, she stayed at the Terrazas home for several days. She was examined by a doctor and was seen by several priests, but no one was able to discover what was causing her problems. It seemed that Norma Moore had attracted a poltergeist. While she was in the Terrazas home, very unusual things occurred: a large wardrobe in Virginia and Francisco's bedroom simply fell over; two rocks fell from the ceiling (out of nowhere) onto a bed while Norma was in the hallway: and a skillet came out of the kitchen, flew around Norma, and went back to the kitchen. Viola, Fresia, Amalia, and Maria Luisa all witnessed these strange occurrences. Since the doctor and priest were unable to diagnose or treat Norma's condition, she was put on a train to California and not heard from again. I have been told that there were newspaper accounts of Norma Moore's stay in Tucson, but I was never able to locate them to confirm the story.

When Zarina Terrazas was around nine years old she had a friend named Kiki who died. Kiki had a bracelet that Zarina had always admired. Shortly after Kiki's death Zarina found the same bracelet in the Terrazas home and was told that Kiki's ghost had probably left it for her. It was thought that Kiki wanted Zarina to die so they could be together to play again. Zarina was not frightened about this because she knew it was a gift from Kiki and was not something to fear, but rather a sign of friendship.

All of these stories have some moral. Ghosts usually appear to people because their motives are to set something right or to help the living. Very rarely did these stories involve ghosts injuring people. Rather, they were there as a warning, a comfort, or to leave a message. They were accepted as part of the culture but one had to be open to them in order to see them or receive their messages. I must admit that I have been frightened of seeing ghosts. But I remember what my cousin Cecilia Dicochea told me, "When you are ready and not afraid, your mother will appear to you and this will be a comfort." I am still waiting.

———•·•———

[1]   Bonnie Henry, *Arizona Daily Star*, 28 October 1987.

CHAPTER 13

Family Tragedies: Los muertos nos recuerdan

No hay mal que por bien no venga.

BIRTH AND DEATH are intimately woven into the fabric of Mexican culture. This was even more the case before the advent of modern medicine. According to the 1900 census, only 63.4 percent of Mexican-American children lived past early childhood in Tucson.[1] Families routinely dealt with death and the grief process was a part of their lives. The Mexican-American families that lived in Tucson had many funeral customs and mores and to disrespect them was not tolerated. Funeral practices change with the times, but there are specific customs that have continued.

In the Mexican culture, death can completely incapacitate a family. Children in the early 1900s were introduced to this process continuously. There was always a fatalistic undercurrent and a feeling that only God controlled one's life. God decided when and what would happen to each person. Individuals merely took part of a supreme plan. Today this would be considered existentialism or an external locus of control.

The first major tragedy that the Urias family remembered was the death of Gilberto in 1925. Celia Diaz and Lupe Urias have gone over this event in detail. They insist that their version of his last days is the most correct, primarily because Celia had been allowed to travel with the family that day. It was to have been a special family outing. Brígida drove the family Buick to an out-of-town baseball game. Only four people could fit in the car and Celia felt very lucky to be one of those who could attend. The people that went on the day trip were Gilberto, Brígida, Ignacia, and Celia.

Celia recalled that Gilberto played baseball for the Azteca team. The Azteca Club, which was a social organization, sponsored this team. The baseball team routinely traveled to other towns in southern Arizona to play games. One weekend in mid-September, the Azteca team traveled to Bisbee. On the way back to Tucson, Gilberto developed terrible abdominal pain. Brígida was instructed by Ignacia to drive directly to the family doctor in Tucson. The doctor diagnosed Gilberto as having appendicitis and he was taken to St. Mary's Hospital where he had an appendectomy. Gilberto survived the surgery, was hospitalized for ten to fourteen days, and then went home to recover. Gilberto was only home for three days; he developed peritonitis and was readmitted to the hospital. Because there were no antibiotics at that time, Gilberto did not survive. He died on October 2, 1925, at the age of 16.

The memory of Gilberto's death is very vivid, even today, for his surviving sisters. Gilberto was very well liked and respected by his siblings. They remembered that his death was extremely traumatic for their mother. Maria Muñoz recalled the anguish and desperation in her mother's crying as she approached the door to the family home. Ignacia didn't want to enter the house where she would never again be able to see Gilberto. The eldest children, Brígida and Antonio, had to carry their mother into the house. Ignacia was given *té de azar* (orange blossom tea) to calm her nerves and was put to bed.[2] It was many months before Ignacia was able to move past her grief; Gilberto's death left her heartbroken.

Antonio Urias had been home during Gilberto's surgery, but he decided to travel to Mexico on business once Gilberto had been sent home to recover. Ignacia had his itinerary and he was immediately wired to return home. The family then had to plan Gilberto's funeral. There were specific customs, dictated by both the Catholic Church and the Mexican culture, that had to be fulfilled.

The most immediate concern was preparation of the body by the funeral home. The Reilly family owned a large mortuary that was quite popular with the Mexican-American families in Tucson. The family also had to have an *esquela* written. This was a special obituary notice in the form of a black-edged card and envelope. The cards were hand delivered

Todos los que ha- biéndolo conocido le habeis amado, rogad al Señor a fin de que le abra sus brazos pater- nos y apague el dolor de los que siempre sen- tirán su cruel pérdida.

Una lágrima por los muertos se evapora; una flor sobre su tum- ba se marchita: una oración por su alma llega a Dios.

—San Agustín.

Q. E. P. D.

Hoy a las 2:40 a. m. dejó de existir en el Seno de la Santa Madre Iglesia Católica Apóstolica Romana, el joven

Gilberto Urias,

a la edad de 16 años, 5 meses

Sus padres, hermanos y demás parientes, al participar a usted la triste nueva, le suplican eleve sus oraciones al Todopo- deroso por el descanso eterno del alma del finado, y se sirva a- compañar mañana, a las 9 a. m., su cadáver de la casa que fué su morada, Avenida 6a. al Sur, 720, a la Iglesia de la Santa Cruz en donde se dirá una Misa de Cuerpo presente, y por la tarde a las 4:30 a su sepelio que tendrá verificativo en el ce- menterio Holy Hope.

Por cuyo favor le vivirán eternamente reconocidos.

Tucsón, Arizona, octubre 2 de 1925.

ANTONIO G. URIAS Y FAMILIA.

El duelo se recibe en la Avenida 6a. al Sur, 720, y se des- pide en el Cementerio.

Esquela of Gilberto Urias.   *1925*

to relatives and family friends. In Gilberto's case, his brothers were required to deliver the notices. Extra esquelas were kept in the home and could be taken by mourners. Esquelas typically had a prayer on one side of the card with a description of the deceased and information about the funeral services on the other side. Celia and Lupe Urias have an original esquela from Gilberto's funeral, as they were important remembrances of departed loved ones.

After the mortuary prepared the body, it was returned to the home for the reviewal. The open casket was usually placed in the largest room of the home and a vigil was kept over the body for a whole day. This was known as the *velorio* (wake). It was not uncommon for people to stay up all night with the deceased. A mass and the funeral were held the following day.

In Gilberto's case, the funeral mass was held at Santa Cruz Church. According to the Urias family, Gilberto's funeral procession was one of the largest held by the Reilly Funeral Home. Gilberto belonged to the El Centro Club at Santa Cruz church and the members accompanied the hearse on foot to Speedway and Main. At that point they were persuaded to get into cars and ride to Holy Hope Cemetery.

After the funeral there was a *novenario* (nine days of praying a novena, a rosary, and prayers) for the repose of the soul of the deceased. Novenarios were held in the evenings. Relatives and friends would gather in the home of the deceased to pray, socialize, and comfort the bereaved. The wake, funeral, and novenario were the first rituals held for the deceased and their family members. Maria Muñoz felt that the novenario served as a social function and thought it was a beautiful tradition. The family of the deceased (*los dolientes*) had the company and comfort of friends and relatives.

There were many mores following a death in Mexican-American families in Tucson during the early 1900s. The period of mourning extended for exactly one year and was strictly observed. Shortly after a person's death, the doorway of the home displayed a black rosette. All of the mirrors inside the home were covered with black cloth. Pianos and other musical instruments were not to be played for a one-year period. The curtains of the home were drawn and there was to be as little sunlight and noise in the home as possible. Men were to wear a black armband on their right arms. Women wore plain black dresses, black slips, and plain black *tapalos,* shawls that allowed only a small area of the face to be shown. Women were able to leave the home to go to mass or to the cemetery. The one-year grieving period enveloped the surviving family in a cocoon of quiet and solitude. It enabled them to adjust to life without the deceased and to gradually reenter society.

Although these customs had been altered by the time I was a child in the 1960s, there were still certain rules that one followed. I found them very stifling and couldn't imagine how people could have endured such rigid practices. In the 1960s the wake and rosary were held at the mortuary the evening before the funeral. After the funeral radios and television were not to be played in the home of the deceased. The home itself was to be kept dark and quiet. Children were not to make any noise out of respect for the bereaved. The nine-day novenario was replaced with an evening of socializing in remembrance of the deceased.

After my parents died (in the 1990s) the earlier mourning practices made complete sense to me. The one-year grieving process allowed people to withdraw into themselves, to suffer privately, and then to carry on their lives, which had been altered by surviving the death of a loved one. I felt that I needed time to adjust; I had to tolerate the sadness and the pain of grief. Silence and shadows fit my mood and were necessary to help me work through the loss.

In 1929 Miguel Terrazas, who had been living with the Urias family, was found dead in bed. Ignacia had been to church early in the morning and returned to prepare breakfast for the family. Since Miguel didn't eat with the family, Ignacia took his breakfast into his room. She was shocked to find him lifeless in bed. Although this was another family tragedy, it wasn't as devastating to Ignacia as it was to her sister Lupe Terrazas. Tía Lupita had waited on Miguel and taken care of him for fifteen years. Again the Terrazas family was summoned to the funeral. Antonio Urias paid Miguel's funeral expenses and he was buried next to Gilberto in the Holy Hope Cemetery. Interestingly enough, no one remembered Tío Miguel's funeral, only the circumstances of his death were mentioned. Tía Lupita continued to live with the Urias family.

Tragedy again struck the Urias family in 1930. The country was in the midst of the Depression. Brígida was the eldest child in the Urias family and assumed many responsibilities of helping her mother. She loved music and was proficient at playing the piano. As the eldest, Brígida learned to drive the first car the family purchased, a Buick. She was responsible for taking her father to Nogales for his business trips and meeting him on his return. The Urias family suffered a huge blow the previous year when Antonio lost his job; the Krupp Company had gone bankrupt due to the Depression.

In the early part of the year, Brígida developed a persistent cough. Ignacia was unable to persuade her to see a doctor. Because her father was out of work, she didn't want to create any expenses. Finally, her parents insisted that she see a doctor. She was taken to see Dr. Thomas, was examined, and sent immediately to the hospital. Ignacia wouldn't tell her younger daughters what Brígida's diagnosis was. Her eyes were red from crying and she would speak in whispers to her friends who attempted to console her. There was a great deal of anxiety in the home due to Ignacia's secrecy and the younger children thought their sister had tuberculosis. In fact, Brígida had developed breast cancer.

Brígida and the Urias family had many friends who helped them through the difficult time. Brígida had a bilateral mastectomy and radium treatments were started. This was very new for medicine in the 1930s. Her younger siblings were rarely permitted to visit her while she was in St. Mary's Hospital. Ignacia stayed with her and came home only in the evenings. Relatives and friends would wait for her on the porch or lawn to hear of Brígida's progress. However, the prognosis was extremely guarded and after being hospitalized for six weeks Brígida succumbed to breast cancer on July 14, 1930.

Upon Brígida's death, Ignacia arrived home from St. Mary's Hospital with piercing cries of anguish.[3] Again there was a wake in the home on South Sixth Avenue. Brígida's casket was placed in the front room before the fireplace and the entire room was filled with flowers and wreaths. Maria Muñoz related that one wreath in particular remained in her memory. A neighbor, Oscar Salvatierra, sent a wreath in the shape of a harp as a memorial to Brígida's love of music. His father had taught many of the Urias children to play the piano.

A novenario followed the funeral and many family friends and relatives filled the Urias home. Ignacia again went into mourning for one year. The deaths of two of her children had been devastating for her. To lose a parent or sibling is tragic, but for a parent to lose children at such young ages is an almost impossible recovery. Antonio and Ignacia Urias were enveloped in sadness.

Angelita Martinez, the mother of Virginia Terrazas, passed away on Feb. 26, 1934, at the age of 72. Viola Terrazas, who was six years old at the time, couldn't remember the circumstances leading to her death. She said that Mi Lande had been very old and frail. However, Viola vaguely recalled the velorio. She said that when the Tucson Mortuary brought the coffin into their home on South Stone Avenue, there was great difficulty maneuvering it through the front door and into the living room. It had been unnerving for her, as a young child, to have her grandmother's corpse displayed in the front room of the family home. Viola said that the other thing she remembered was that the strong scent of the flowers in the room had been overpowering. The intense floral scents were necessary to mask the deterioration of the body. To this day, she can't tolerate the smell of gardenias.

Angelita Martinez (Maria de los Angeles Martinez) was buried in Holy Hope Cemetery. I tried to locate her headstone as Cecelia Dicochea had an old photograph the family had taken. I was unable to find it and was told by personal at the cemetery that many headstones in the old part of the cemetery had sunk into the earth. Many of those graves are unmarked today.

I can remember my mother, Amalia, speaking not of her grandmother's funeral, but of her sister Zarina's reaction. Zarina had been very close to Angelita and took her death quite hard. Zarina would have been eighteen at the time and her grandmother had cared for her since infancy. Zarina was unable to speak due to the trauma. The Urias sisters recollected that Francisco Terrazas asked their mother if Zarina could stay with them. They felt that she was with them for only several days before she regained her composure and began speaking.

The final significant blow to families was the death of Antonio Urias. Antonio never recovered from the emotional and financial devastation of his job loss during the Depression. Gilberto and Brígida's deaths had also taken an emotional toll on him. A final straw had been losing the beloved family home on South Sixth Avenue in January 1931. They had had to move to a much smaller home on Penn Place just north of downtown Tucson.

Maria Muñoz recounted an incident that happened to her when she was walking home after classes at the University of Arizona. When

Tucson (Nov: 3, 1918 - 10 a.m.)

Antonio and Ignacia Urias.   1918

PHOTO COURTESY OF ARIZONA HISTORICAL SOCIETY, TUCSON
Courtesy of the Arizona Historical Society/Tucson. 91655

Maria got to 2nd and South 6th she saw two older women walking toward her. They were wearing long black skirts and their heads were covered with black tapalos. She felt overwhelming grief and realized that something tragic was going to occur. She felt that seeing the women had been a vision and she could not escape the feeling that it was a portent of doom.

Ignacia had been treating Antonio for stomach discomfort with bicarbonate of soda for several days. On January 24, 1934, Antonio had been forced to sign over the mortgage of his old family home on 135

Cushing. He had tenants living in the house and, because it was the Depression, they had been negligent in paying the rent. Due to the stress the family had experienced that day, they all went to bed early. The girls were awakened by their mother's grief-stricken voice crying, "Ay, Antonio." They knew something horrible had happened. Their father had died in bed after retiring at about 10 P.M. Maria always wondered if the stress of signing the Cushing Street property over to the bank contributed to her father's death.

A wake was held in the home on Penn Place the night of January 25 and the interment was the next day. Several Terrazas cousins went to the Urias home early in the morning of the 25th to help comfort their cousins. At intervals the bereaved were served té de azar to calm their nerves. Afterward, a novenario was held in the home. Friends and relatives arrived to pray for Antonio's soul and to comfort his family.

The death of her husband was a shock to Ignacia Urias. However, she was described as being very brave following his death. She didn't become as morose as she had following the deaths of Gilberto and Brígida. She had suffered so much pain following the deaths of her children that she had come to accept the fact that death was part of the life process. Her spiritual beliefs helped her believe that they would be reunited at some point in the future.

Part of my research required that I review records from Holy Hope Cemetery. This was a place that I had feared since childhood. Even now, I feel some trepidation when passing by the cemetery. I remember my mother and Aunt Zarina taking their children there on All Soul's Day. We were to go there out of respect after attending mass. We went to the gravesites of my grandparents where we were required to say prayers. My mother and aunt always cried as they left flowers. Afterward we went to the old section of the cemetery, which I found very frightening. There was little grass in the old section. The markers weren't well kept and many were leaning or even sinking into the plots. But must horrifying of all were those sites with holes going underneath the headstones. My mother and aunt told us that ground squirrels had dug tunnels under the headstones. With our vivid imaginations we children were afraid that a skeleton would reach up and grab our feet. We walked up and down the rows trying to find the headstone of Angelita Martinez as Zarina and my mother had forgotten where her plot was located. I still have nightmares of wandering through the dusty rows of gravesites in this old section.

When I contacted personnel at Holy Hope Cemetery, I did so with the intention of obtaining dates of death for Brígida, Miguel, and Altagracia Terrazas. But I was given much more information than I had expected. Patricia Portillo was graciously able to supply me with both information about the cemetery and maps of family burial sites. This in turn helped me find more accurate information about dates of birth and death of family predecessors.

Miguel and Altagracia Terrazas were most probably buried in the Court Street Cemetery, which was located between Speedway Boulevard and Second Street. When real estate values increased in the early 1900s, the city council elected to stop burials after 1908 and move the remains to the new Holy Hope or Evergreen Cemeteries.[4] I was always told that Evergreen Cemetery was for Protestants and Holy Hope was for Catholics. In fact, Evergreen is divided into sections for many denominations while Holy Hope is entirely Catholic.

Ms. Portillo indicated that Miguel and Altagracia's remains were probably buried together at Holy Hope after 1910. Ms. Portillo was able to give me a map with locations for the Terrazas and Urias family members. Those family members who died before 1950 were buried in the oldest portion of the cemetery, blocks F and B. Celia Diaz and Lupe Urias indicated that burial sites were bought in blocks. Therefore, family members who died within short periods of time were buried together, while those who died later were buried in different locations. The early family burial sites, those of Brígida, Miguel, and Altagracia Terrazas, have no current tombstones. Maria de los Angeles Martinez is said to have a headstone, but none was located. The Urias family members all have headstones and are buried fairly close to each other.

One final tidbit of information, which I find quite interesting but also fairly discriminatory, is the placement of plots in Holy Hope. According to Fred McAninch, when Holy Hope was planned all gravesites were placed in a north to south direction. It was felt that since most of those buried in the old sections were of Mexican-American descent, their bodies were placed facing their "homeland of Mexico." Christian and Jewish burial practices typically orient gravesites east and west. The plots in the newer sections of the cemetery are laid out this way.[5]

Although these deaths were tragic for both the Urias and Terrazas families, they were not unusual. The reactions and customs surrounding the funeral process were observed rituals among the Mexican-American inhabitants of Tucson at that time. I feel that these customs and the cultural attitudes towards death have served to create a sense of negativity towards the outlook on the future. Death, the process of dying, and funeral practices continue to be ingrained in Mexican-Americans' fatalistic attitude toward life.

In spite of this fatalistic approach to life, the attitude toward death and the customs relating to it are of great benefit. As with everything else, customs change with the times. Some practices are deleted and others are added. The length of the grieving process, for example, is much shorter now. However, it is important to remember the practices of our ancestors in order to understand why certain things are done today.

---

[1] Sheridan, *Los Tucsonenses*, 135.

[2] Muñoz interview, 3 May 1997.

[3] Ibid.

[4] Bonnie Henry, *Arizona Daily Star*, 11 September 1990.

[5] Fred McAninch, interview by Michal Davenport, 17 November 1995.

CHAPTER 14

The Depression

Ya estoy arta de todo esto.

THE COLLAPSE of the New York stock market on October 29, 1929, brought difficult times not only for the nation and state, but also for the city of Tucson. By the following year the city was beginning to feel the economic problems that were affecting the rest of the nation. The population of the city at that time was roughly 32,000.[1] Although the population of Tucson had continued to increase, Mexican-American citizens had become a minority in the town.

During the 1920s Mexicans represented only 37 percent of Tucson's population.[2] This was the start of a trend that would continue into the next several decades. The Depression was more of an economic problem for the Mexican-American citizens than for their Anglo counterparts. The Arizona legislature had limited Mexican immigration in 1929. The economic crisis forced many immigrants back to Mexico while others became unemployed. Most people held on to their jobs for as long as they were available. Those who were self-employed simply attempted to keep their businesses afloat.

During the Depression many Mexican-American families in Tucson began migrating to California. Both the Urias and Terrazas families had relatives who had moved to Los Angeles in search of better jobs. Occasionally these relatives would drift back to Tucson. Cousins often lived with relatives in Tucson while their parents worked in California. Celia Diaz recalled that Ignacia Urias took in a young cousin and that Angelita Martinez took in a great-niece into the Terrazas home. Both of these children had parents who lived in Los Angeles. Once they were financially able, they came back to reclaim the children.

Antonio Urias lost his job with the Hayman Krupp Company in 1931. He was out of work for almost three years before being hired as a laborer for the Work Progress Administration (WPA). The man who had been a dry goods salesman willingly took a job as a laborer building highways. The Urias family had suffered the illness and death of Brígida and because of his poor job situation, Antonio had been forced to borrow money to cover expenses. The financial situation became increasingly difficult as the tenant of a property he and Ignacia owned on Cushing Street failed to pay rent. In 1933 the family was forced to move from their home on South 6th Avenue to a much smaller home on Penn Place, which was north of downtown. It was very difficult for the family to move from their beautiful home that had been so full of wonderful memories. The home on Penn Place was much smaller and socially was a step down for the Urias family. Although the Depression affected the family financially, they never lacked food, shelter, and their positive home life.

Antonio Urias was not accustomed to the manual work necessary for his WPA job. It was difficult both physically and emotionally. Maria Muñoz believed it was humiliating for a man who had provided well for his family to be relegated to that type of work. The stressors of his daughter's illness and death and losing the home on South 6th Avenue and the property on 135 Cushing lead to his untimely death in 1934.

For the Urias family, the Depression came to signify a complete change in what to that point had been a wonderful lifestyle. During the 1930s they lost a sister, father, and home. Life became more difficult, but the family was helped by the support of their Tía Lupita. She owned properties on Bean Street and South 3rd Avenue and was able to contribute a portion of the income she earned from rents. The older Urias children found jobs to help support the family – many times at the expense of continuing advanced education. Ignacia Urias was good at making ends meet and although the family went through many hardships, they were able to survive the Depression years.

The Terrazas family fared somewhat better. They continued to live in the home on South Stone Avenue. Owning a small grocery store proved to be very beneficial, as they never were lacking for food. The whole family was involved in the operation of the store. Fresia Lindberg recalled that during the Depression the family would go to the store in

Terrazas Grocery, 273 South Convent.   *c. 1930*
PHOTO COURTESY OF VIOLA TERRAZAS

the mornings, eat breakfast together, and help get orders ready for delivery. After school they would return to the store and help with whatever tasks had to be done.[3] My mother, Amalia Goodman, related to me that she never recalled the Depression as a hardship for her family. Since her father had the store they always had food, clothes, and a roof over their heads. She said that her father couldn't stand to see people go hungry and he often allowed customers to buy groceries on credit.

The Depression years did constitute a hardship for Angelita Martinez. She had Virginia Terrazas' family and her granddaughter, Carlota Tena, living with her in the home on South Stone. Another daughter, Maria Cienfuegos, along with her husband, Apolonio, lived in a small home on the property. The mystery of the ownership of this home has been a cause for much suffering and concern over the years. Although deeds exist that indicate Angelita purchased and owned the property, there has been no evidence found showing Virginia Terrazas as an owner of the home.

At this point in time the ownership of the Terrazas family home is a moot issue. However, I feel I must somehow clarify the situation and perhaps diffuse some of the anger Virginia Terrazas' children directed at her.

The mystery surrounding the ownership of the house on South Stone unravels if one considers the property tax laws of that time. Initially the home did belong to Angelita Martinez and Carlota Tena. However, like many homeowners during the Depression, at some point Angelita Martinez was probably unable to pay the property taxes on the home and was at risk of losing the property.

If Virginia agreed to pay back taxes on the property, the home would have become hers. The conclusion I have drawn is that because she paid the taxes for her mother, Virginia Terrazas saved the family home and became the rightful owner of the home when Angelita died in 1934.

I do not have the ability to explain my grandmother's actions to her children. I can only hope to identify the fact that her actions enabled her family to retain their home at a time when so many other families were losing property. I did not know her well enough to voice her opinions, but with her assertive personality she probably did not feel that she owed anyone an explanation concerning her actions or business dealings. What is important for the descendants of Francisco and Virginia Terrazas to remember is that Virginia did what she felt she had to do in order to keep her family intact and maintain a home in which to live. For that we must forgive her and our parents and honor the fact that she had the strength and commitment needed to keep her home for her family.

Though the descendants of Francisco and Virginia did not recall experiencing many of the traumas that struck other Mexican-American families in Tucson during the Depression, I feel the family did in fact suffer. Francisco Terrazas cannot be described as an assertive man. He overextended credit to many people within the Mexican-American community. This caused a great deal of stress and friction between him and Virginia. As a result his business was in a very tenuous position during the Depression years. The Terrazas grocery store was able to stay in business but the next decade would put even more stress on the financial condition.

Mexican-American families in Tucson function in large extended-family networks. In both the Terrazas and Urias families the expectation was that all family members who were able would contribute to the financial well-being of the family. Any unmarried member who had graduated from high school was expected to work and help support the family. Married children were to care for their families first, but were to contribute to the family in some way. Several members of the Urias family had been enrolled in the University of Arizona at the outbreak of the Depression. Celia dropped out of college so that she could help support her family. Lupe and Armida started working immediately after graduating from high school so they could help the family. Maria was the only sibling who was able to attend the university due to financial help from the Dean of Women, Calanthe Brazelton. Antonio, Gonzalo, and Ignacio also worked but because they were married contributed to the family in other ways. They provided financial and emotional support to their younger siblings.

The offspring of Francisco and Virginia Terrazas were all expected to work when they finished high school. Bertha was the only one who worked full time at the family store. What was different for the Terrazas children was that they were required to turn their paychecks over to their mother. She decided the amount of spending money they were able to keep. Unless they were married, the money they earned belonged to the family. This was a bone of contention for Zarina and Amalia, but Maria Luisa felt that it was her responsibility to contribute her earnings to her mother. Virginia controlled the family finances and made the decisions regarding household expenses. Some might argue that this was too controlling. However, she was able to preserve the integrity of the family's property during the difficult Depression years.

There were various social clubs in Tucson during the Depression that helped bolster spirits of the Mexican-American community. The Alianza and Club Azteca raised money to help feed local children. They held dances at the Blue Moon Ballroom, which both the Urias and Terrazas cousins remembered fondly. The newspaper *El Tucsonense* also provided information and support to the Mexican-American community.

Many people in the Mexican-American community in Tucson were taking notice of Franklin Roosevelt. The general feeling was that he was instrumental in ending the Depression and putting people back to work. I remember listening to Ignacia Urias and her friends Mercedes Wood and Anna Maria Heinemann discussing the merits of the Democratic Party, but especially Franklin Roosevelt.

Their feeling was that he had single-handedly moved the country back on track economically. My mother frequently took us to visit her Aunt Ignacia on Sunday afternoons. There in her living room, she and her friends would discuss and debate the Depression, World War II, politics, and their support of Franklin Roosevelt. We children were allowed to sit and quietly listen or play outside while our parents served refreshments and entered into the discussions with the matriarchs.

As the Depression moved to a close, both the Urias and Terrazas families had remained intact, although they both suffered hardships and stress, especially the Urias family. They lost their home, financial stability, and several important members of the family. However, both families worked diligently on enduring the hardships and weathered the national crisis.

———————

1 Sonnichsen, *Tucson*, 280.
2 Sheridan, *Los Tucsonenses*, 184.
3 Lindberg interview, 22 August 1996.

CHAPTER 15

The Prewar Years

Mejor sola que mal acompanada.

FEW U.S. CITIZENS were spared the hardships of the Great Depression and that included the citizens of Tucson. Almost all families had to make sacrifices in order to survive the financial hardships. The one thing that most people gained was a greater sense of community and social awareness.

In 1932 Franklin D. Roosevelt was elected president of the United States. His New Deal policies created programs that gradually spurred the growth of the economy. President Roosevelt was well supported within the Mexican-American enclave of Tucson. The WPA put many *Tucsonenses* back to work. These projects are still in evidence throughout the state of Arizona and include Hoover Dam and the highway system. The Mexican-American citizens of Tucson learned to cope with the Depression and managed to survive with their families and their heritage intact.

The Terrazas and Urias families were no exceptions. Both families made tremendous personal sacrifices. Both families lost crucial family members, though this was more true of the Urias family. By the late 1930s the majority of the children in both families had reached their teens and early twenties. The financial hardships of the Depression years meant that many of these young adults were unable to continue their educations. Almost all of these young people graduated from Tucson High School but the majority were unable to go to college. The family expectation was that they were to obtain jobs and help support the extended family.

The cohesiveness of Mexican families is still evident. The extended family is of primary importance. Family members may argue and disagree but there remains the strong theme and pull of family. As heads of the household, the parents held the family together and demanded ultimate respect. Both Virginia and Francisco Terrazas directed their children. In the Urias family the children turned to Ignacia, but at the same time had to provide emotional support following the death of Antonio.

During the late 1930s most of the young adults in the Terrazas and Urias families held clerical or sales positions in the larger businesses in Tucson. These included Jacome's, Steinfelds, and the newspapers (both *The Star* and *The Citizen*). My mother, Amalia Terrazas Goodman, worked at Ruben Gold's store as a bookkeeper immediately after graduating from high school. Her brother Francisco (Frank) was encouraged to attend the University of Arizona. The three youngest Terrazas siblings continued their basic education.

I can remember my mother saying that her parents never led her or her siblings to believe that the Depression years had been a total hardship. She felt that because the family owned a store they were spared the misfortune of being hungry or without a home. They survived because of the resourcefulness of their parents. Work had to come first in order to sustain the family, but there was also time for recreation. My mother's fondest recollections of the late Depression years were of the Carnegie Library, the movie theaters, and the Blue Moon Ballroom.

The old Military Plaza had been developed in the early part of the 1900s into Armory Park, The Santa Rita Hotel, and the Carnegie Library. In 1900 the library was built with funds from the Carnegie Foundation. Located in Library Park on South 6th Avenue between East 12th and East 13th Streets, it was built in the French Renaissance style and trimmed in terra cotta and cast stone. In 1939 wings were added on each side of the original building. One wing was reserved for children and the other for adults. Each wing had a large patio that could be used for outdoor reading.[1] The people of Tucson were very proud of the library.

The Carnegie Library was one of my mother's favorite places. She loved the cool reading areas where she could lose herself in a book. Reading was an escape for her. Through reading she was able to travel and learn about history and famous people. The library offered her refuge and a chance to explore the world and life through various authors. Her family couldn't afford to buy books so her library card became an important possession. Her favorite stories were *Rebecca of Sunnybrook Farm*, *Little Women*, and *The Five Little Peppers and How They Grew*. She was often described as a bookworm and people told her that the reason she had such poor vision was because she read so much.

My mother passed on her love of reading to me. I remember her taking me to the Carnegie Library and quietly walking through the building. She said we had to take care not to disturb other readers. The building seemed immense and impressive, my footsteps echoed on its floors. It was very cool and still and somewhat like a tomb. I enjoyed the grounds surrounding the building, with their expansive lawn and towering palm trees. I never spent much time there because it was not close

Standing, left to right: Fresia, Rene, Zarina, Bertha, Amalia, Viola, Delia, Maria Luisa, Frank. *Seated:* Virginia and Francisco Terrazas. *c. 1942*
PHOTO COURTESY OF VIOLA TERRAZAS

to my family's home. We visited my grandmother often and although the library was a very short walk from her home on South Stone, we rarely visited the building. I found it intimidating and preferred the smaller library at Himmel Park. But for my mother, the Carnegie Library was a place of great importance during both her childhood and early adult years.

Another diversion for the Terrazas and Urias families was the theater. Tucson had a variety of theaters. In the early 1900s El Teatro Carmen and El Teatro Royal were popular with the Mexican-American citizens. These theaters were located on Meyer Street between Cushing and McCormick streets. Both theaters hosted companies of Mexican actors who performed plays or vaudeville acts in Spanish. The Opera and Rialto were theaters that were attended by the Anglo citizens of Tucson.

Later, moving picture theaters became popular. Most of these theaters were located on Congress. The Fox, Lyric, State, Plaza (which showed movies in Spanish), and Paramount theaters provided a means of escape during the Depression. Not only was this true for the people of Tucson, but for a large number of people throughout the United States. Movies were an escape mechanism that provided animated works, comedies, and musicals. During the summer and on Saturdays the Terrazas and Urias cousins would attend matinees. Their favorites included Mickey Mouse, The Little Rascals, and Laurel and Hardy. As the Depression dragged on and the cousins moved through adolescence, their tastes changed to musicals. Through these films they were able to lose themselves for an afternoon and were transported to a more hopeful, glamorous world.

After attending the movies it was popular to walk to the Palace of Sweets or Sam's Place where there were soda fountains. There they could have cones, ice cream sodas, sundaes, or soft drinks. The next destination before going home was to window shop. One might not be able to afford things, but it didn't cost anything to look at the beautiful displays. The cousins would stroll past Jacome's, Steinfelds, Levy's, and Ronstadt's. Other shops that they found interesting were the Borgaro Indian Store, Rebeil's (which sold appliances), and Dave Bloom (a men's clothing store).

As the Terrazas and Urias cousins moved into young adulthood, the

Blue Moon Ballroom became a favorite meeting place. The Blue Moon was located at 1415 North Oracle. It was in operation from 1920 to 1947. The ballroom was described by Maria Muñoz as a large building that looked much like a barn. It was made of sheets of corrugated tin and constructed so that sections of the tin could be raised for ventilation. When the two opposite sides were lifted it became an open-air building. Benches were placed lengthwise along the walls of the building so people could sit until they were asked to dance.

The Blue Moon was well known to the cousins as it had been a favorite with their parents and with many members of the Mexican-American community. In the 1920s Francisco and Virginia Terrazas enjoyed going there to dance. Their children remembered them as being beautiful dancers. Sunday afternoons were considered Mexican-American day. *Tardeadas*, social events that included dancing, were organized on Sunday afternoons but were later moved to the evening. The Alianza Hispano-Americana and other Mexican-American groups leased the ballroom on Sunday nights.[2]

During the Depression the Blue Moon became even more important to the Mexican-American citizens of Tucson. Not only was the Blue Moon important to their social lives, but it provided service events. The Club Latino organized a series of dances in the spring of 1930 to raise money to provide free lunches for children at Ochoa School. This was one of the earliest charitable efforts of the Mexican-American community in Tucson during the Depression.[3]

When the Urias and Terrazas cousins were adolescents they would sit in their parents' cars, listen to the music, and watch the dancers. In their late-teen years they were finally allowed to go to the Blue Moon. They were only allowed to go as a group as that was what was socially acceptable. Delia Terrazas related to Maria Muñoz that when the Terrazas girls asked for permission to go to the Blue Moon their mother would answer, "Si van las Urias pueden ir." ("If the Uriases are going you may go.") Their group was described as well behaved and sensible.

It is important to realize that etiquette was very important in the Mexican-American community, especially for young ladies. Young women were never allowed to go out by themselves. They either went out as a group or with a chaperone (who could have been a mother, aunt, or older female relative). It was not socially acceptable to be out alone especially with a young man. This was especially true when attending events at the Blue Moon. Even when asked to dance, the young women were closely observed.

In general, Sundays continued to be important days for families to socialize. Many families continued to host gatherings that included food, singing, dancing, and card games. These gatherings were not as elaborate as those of the 1910s and 1920s. They continued to function as a means of conveying a sense of family as well as offering a forum for discussion of politics and social issues.

As the United States moved toward the close of the 1930s and of the Depression, the threat of war in Europe loomed on the horizon. The citizens of Tucson were not immune from the fears of the rest of the country. The major difference it meant for the Urias and Terrazas families was that the political events now had a major impact on those members born after 1910. They were now adults and would be involved in the consequences of war.

---

1   Miller, Joseph. *Arizona: The Grand Canyon State. A State Guide.* The American Guide Series. (New York: Hastings House Publishers, 1966), 259.

2   Bonnie Henry, "Another Tucson," *Arizona Daily Star*, 1992.

3   Sheridan, *Los Tucsonenses*, 213.

CHAPTER 16

The 1940s

Bendición

THE 1940S AND WORLD WAR II brought societal changes to the United States. Tucson was not exempt from these changes. By 1940 the population of Tucson had reached almost 37,000 and roughly 30 percent were Mexican-American. Women became an instrumental part of the work force and their roles changed. They became slightly more independent. This meant many changes for the Mexican-American community of Tucson. No longer were our mothers content to give all their earnings back to the extended family. They questioned their parents' authority and values and wanted their sheltered lives somewhat updated. Tucson itself was changing into a larger, more cosmopolitan city, and the young adults changed with the times. The generation of Francisco and Virginia Terrazas and Antonio and Ignacia Urias was giving way to their children's generation.

By the beginning of the 1940s the Terrazas and Urias cousins were beginning to marry and start families of their own. Most had finished Tucson High School and were working in Tucson. Those that were unmarried were expected to contribute their earnings to support the family. Because the Urias family had no male head of household, the married children financially contributed to their mother and younger siblings. This was what was expected and part of what it meant to be family.

Carlota Tena had married Emilio Pompa, a rancher in Sonora. Their marriage didn't work out and was annulled by the Church. Carlota returned to Tucson and the home of her Terrazas relatives. She was employed by Steinfelds department store until she moved to Los Angeles for better financial opportunities. She continued to claim that the home on Stone Avenue actually belonged to her since her grandmother, Angelita Martinez, had purchased it with her "inheritance." What she didn't mention was that Virginia and Francisco Terrazas had probably paid the property taxes, utilities, and kept up the home.

None of the Terrazas family spoke much about Maria Cinfuegos

Amalia Terrazas and Guadalupe Urias (seated) in
Mexico City with friends.   *c. 1943*
PHOTO COURTESY OF LUPE URIAS

(Prietita) or her husband Apolonio. They continued to live in the small bungalow behind the main house on Stone Avenue through the 1930s. They eventually bought a home of their own several blocks west of Stone Avenue in the Barrio Anita district. Although Virginia and Maria saw each other, they were not particularly close. The Terrazas family rarely saw the Cienfuegos socially. No one ever commented on the death of Apolonio. It was just known that after his death Prietita became more isolated and strange. One of the saddest discoveries was that Prietita died of dementia alone in the state mental institution in Phoenix.

Many young men from Tucson went to war and they served their country proudly. Frank entered the Army and served in the South Pacific. He was wounded in action, but recovered. The family was elated when the war ended and Frank returned home. Rene entered the Navy at the end of the war, but never went overseas. Their sisters, like so many other women, toiled with their jobs at home.

Francisco Terrazas was able to keep his small grocery store open during the Depression. However, he extended too much credit to customers during that time and was forced to close the store. For a few years during the 1940s he ran an extremely small business out of the home on South Stone Avenue. Viola Terrazas remembered the shelving and goods that lined the walls of one of the small front rooms of their home. His small venture was even less profitable and he was finally forced to close even that. This produced a great deal of marital stress between him and Virginia. Francisco eventually took a job tending bar at the Sports Club and became fairly despondent. The relationship between him and Virginia continued to deteriorate.

Tucson in the 1940s had changed from the small dusty community that it had been into a quickly growing city with an expanding population and a thriving economy. What has not changed is knowing that although life for us is different than it was for our parents, grandparents, and great-grandparents, we still share the basic theme of family. Tucson has continued to be a Hispanic community – one with great veneration for its forefathers. Tucson is unique in that the Mexican-American community still fosters its original culture and customs. We have been taught to be proud of our heritage and to pass it to our children. Yes, we lead different lives than our parents, but our values continue to be the same. These are the memories of our past that we wish to pass on to future generations. Do not forget from whom or where you have come, this is a theme that has been handed down and that we will continue to teach.

I have recorded many of the memories of our Terrazas family. I have rediscovered many forgotten items and I have passed on the basis for many family traditions. What they gave us were memories of that era and the era of their parents. It was a much different, quiet time. These are the memories that have been saved and recorded. (It will be up to the next generation to record the next set of memories.) Many of these recorded events were important to our mothers, fathers, cousins, and aunts. There are some things I was not able to discover, science has not moved that quickly yet, but it will soon. Alzheimer's Disease does affect our family. Many of our parents had the malady: Virginia Terrazas and Maria Cienfuegos were called senile. I was unable to find people on the Urias side of the family with this illness. It leads me to believe that Maria de los Angeles Martinez was probably the carrier. However, no one remembers her as being senile.

Science is making many advances on causes and treatments for Alzheimer's Disease. Many of those in our family lost their memories and lives to this disease of deterioration. Let us not forget that which they were able to leave for us. They have been our teachers, mentors, and confidants. They are our past, we are their present, and our children are the future. We owe our life circle to our forefathers and foremothers and must in turn pass it on to our children. This is their history, these are their memories.

Left to right: Ignacia Urias, Francisco Terrazas, Sara Castelan, Guadalupe
Terrazas.   1954

PHOTO COURTESY OF VIOLA TERRAZAS

To order additional copies of *Recuerdos*:

Web: www.itascabooks.com

Phone: 1-800-901-3480

Fax: Copy and fill out the form below with credit card information. Fax to 763-398-0198

Mail: Copy and fill out the form below. Mail with check or credit card information to:

Syren Book Company
5120 Cedar Lake Road
Minneapolis, Minnesota 55416

Order Form

Copies	Title / Author	Price	Totals	
	Recuerdos / Elizabeth McCauslin	$14.95	$	
	Subtotal		$	
	7% sales tax (MN only)		$	
	Shipping and handling, first copy		$	4.00
	Shipping and handling, ___ add'l copies @$1.00 ea.		$	
	TOTAL TO REMIT		$	

Payment Information:

__ Check Enclosed __ Visa/MasterCard		
Card number:	Expiration date:	
Name on card:		
Billing address:		
City:	State:	Zip:
Signature :	Date:	

Shipping Information:

__ Same as billing address __ Other (enter below)		
Name:		
Address:		
City:	State:	Zip: